OREGON
Nature Weekends

by Jim Yuskavitch

FALCON®

HELENA, MONTANA

A FALCON GUIDE®

Falcon® Publishing is continually expanding its list of recreational guidebooks. All books include detailed descriptions, accurate maps, and all information necessary for enjoyable trips. You can order extra copies of this book and get information and prices for other Falcon® books by writing Falcon, P.O. Box 1718, Helena, MT 59624, or by calling toll-free 1-800-582-2665. Also, please ask for a copy of our current catalog. Visit our website at www.Falcon.com or contact us by e-mail at falcon@falcon.com.

1 2 3 4 5 6 7 8 9 0 MG 05 04 03 02 01 00

All black-and-white photos by the author unless otherwise noted.

Cover photo of waterfall at the back of the aorae, Oneonta Gorge by Tom Bol.
Cover photo of wildlife viewing at Hart Mountain National Antelope Refuge by Fred Pflughoft.
Cover photo of pacific tree frog by Jim Yuskavitch.
Back cover photo of sunflowers at Tom McCall Preserve by Dan Sherwood.

Library of Congress Cataloging-in-Publication Data
Yuskavitch, James
    Oregon Nature Weekends / by Jim Yuskavitch
       p. cm.
    ISBN 1-56044-964-0
    1. Natural history--Oregon--Guidebooks. 2. Wildlife
watching--Oregon--Guidebooks.
    3. Oregon--Guidebooks. I. Title.

    QH105.07 Y87 2000
    508.795--dc21   00-039385

Project Editor: Gayle Shirley
Copyeditor: Shana Harrington
Page Compositor: Jeff Wincapaw
Book and cover design by Jeff Wincapaw

CAUTION

Outdoor recreational activities are by their very nature potentially hazardous. All participants in such activities must assume responsibility for their own actions and safety. The information contained in this guidebook cannot replace sound judgment and good decision-making skills, which help reduce exposure, nor does the scope of this book allow for the disclosure of all the potential hazards and risks involved in such activities.

    Learn as much as possible about the outdoor recreational activities in which you participate, prepare for the unexpected, and be cautious. The reward will be a safer and more enjoyable experience.

♻ Text pages printed on recycled paper.

Contents

Spring

MARCH

APRIL

MAY

Summer

JUNE

JULY

AUGUST

Autumn

Winter

BEST BETS

INDEX

ABOUT THE AUTHOR

NATURE NOTES

Knowing where to go, and when, are the keys to experiencing the wonders of Oregon's natural environment, including the lush rain forest of Cape Perpetua, south of Newport.

Introduction

Leave the lawnmower in the garage this Saturday, and put off that household project for another day. There is something happening every weekend in Oregon's wild and not-so-wild places, and this book will get you there at just the right time. Migrating birds by the thousands, mountain meadows abloom with wildflowers, ponds full of salamanders, whales sounding off the coast, geese honking in the winter sky, bugling elk, and soaring hawks are all part of Oregon's natural repertoire. And just where can you find all these delights of nature? Read on.

How to Use This Book

The nature trips in this book are presented in such a way that you get all the details at a glance: how to get there, when to go, and what you can expect to see and experience when you arrive. You will also find background information on each destination and suggestions of what to do and where exactly to go to get the most out of the experience.

Other helpful information you will find includes any required admission fees and the minimum amount of time you need to see what there is to see, as well as a list of suggested equipment, clothing, and other items you might want to bring along to more fully enjoy your outing. Also included are special tips or precautions specific to each listing, and addresses and phone numbers where you can obtain more information about a destination.

Unless otherwise noted, all the places described in this guide are accessible by standard passenger vehicles with average clearance.

Tips for Nature Explorers

Knowing where to go, and when, are the keys to experiencing the wonders that Oregon's environment offers. That is what this book is all about. But knowing what to do when you get there can make all the difference in the overall quality of your visit. Here are some tips to help you get the most out of each nature outing you take.

This guide contains all the information you need to hop into your car and head for the hills. But there is no substitute for the expertise and experience of the refuge managers, park rangers, and others who work full-time in these areas. Do not be reluctant to call ahead before you start out or to ask questions of staff people who may be available at the site when you arrive. Although most natural events follow predictable cycles and patterns, sometimes they may throw you a curve. Wildlife migrations may run a little off schedule due to unusual environmental conditions. Wildlife activity may temporarily shift from one part of a refuge to another, or warm weather may delay the fall foliage for a week or two. Getting up-to-date information can help you plan your trip for maximum enjoyment and minimum disappointment.

Since many of the sites in this book involve wildlife viewing, a few tips and hints will help increase your success. As a rule, the best times of day to see wild animals are mornings and evenings. There are exceptions, though, which are noted in trip descriptions when they apply. Surprisingly, many wildlife species are less afraid of vehicles than of people, perhaps because they often do not recognize cars and trucks as a threat. As a result, in places where roads pass through wildlife habitat, you will often see more wildlife—and see it from a closer vantage—if you stay in your vehicle. Some wildlife refuges require visitors to remain in their vehicles to avoid disturbing animals during critical times of the year, particularly in areas where waterfowl winter.

Although you really do not need any fancy, expensive equipment to appreciate nature, there are a few items that are handy to have. Binoculars are a standard piece of equipment that will help you get a closer look at critters ranging from bald eagles to butterflies. A spotting scope is very helpful for viewing wildlife in the distance. Cameras and notebooks are useful for recording your experiences for future reference. Other specialty equipment might include a magnifying glass for examining wildflowers and a tape recorder for preserving the sounds of nature.

Field identification guides are indispensable additions to your nature-watching kit. Guides to birds and wildflowers tend to be the most popular and frequently used, but chances are there is a field identification guide available for just about anything in nature that interests you, including insects, mammals, trees, fish, spiders, butterflies, mushrooms, and more.

But the most useful tool in a nature watcher's toolbox is patience. Nature follows its own cycles at its own pace, unconcerned with the increasingly hurried world in which we humans live. When you are out on your weekend excursions, take a deep breath and slow down a bit. Do not rush from viewpoint to viewpoint trying to "make time." If the wildlife you have come to see is not there when you arrive, wait around awhile. Although each trip description suggests a minimum amount of time to spend, you are bound to see more the longer you stay.

Be Prepared

A famous Arctic explorer once said that adventures in the wilderness were usually the result of poor planning or poor judgment. His point was that when you are in the outdoors you do not want to have any "adventures." You want things to go smoothly, as they were planned. Although the trips in this book will not take you into the wilderness, some will take you a bit off the beaten path. To avoid having any unplanned adventures on your outings, take some basic precautions and use a touch of common sense.

First, dress for the weather and always be prepared for the worst. This means that you should not assume the weather will be nice for your entire trip, even if it is the middle of the summer and sunny and warm when you set out. Cold and rain can blow onto the Oregon coast at any time of year. Mountain areas can be hit with unexpected snowstorms. And nighttime temperatures often plummet in the High Desert country, even in the summer.

Dressing in layers is an effective technique. It allows you to control your level of comfort by adding or subtracting items of clothing depending on weather conditions and your level of exertion. A typical layering scheme in the winter, for example, is wool or polypropylene underwear, a wool shirt, a fleece coat, and a waterproof rain parka, along with a wool or fleece cap and gloves. In the summer, you might want to include lightweight pants and a jacket along with shorts and a T-shirt. Sturdy (although not necessarily heavy) hiking boots are generally better than sneakers or running shoes for negotiating trails. And hats are an important item year-round. They ward off sun in the summer and rain and snow in the winter. Having adequate clothing to cope with unexpected (as well as expected) inclement weather can make all the difference between a pleasant and a not-so-pleasant outing. And do not forget some food and liquids—even if you anticipate a short excursion.

Take the same approach to planning your driving trip. When taking trips to snow country, be prepared for winter driving conditions by bringing tire chains along. Flares are a good idea, too—just in case. And do not forget to check road conditions before leaving home. When you travel in the desert areas of eastern Oregon during the summer, it is not a bad idea to have some extra jugs of water along. You can drink the water or put it in your radiator if your car begins overheating.

When visiting some of the more out-of-the-way areas described in this book, inquire locally about current road conditions. Roads in remote areas that were perfectly good last year may have been washed out by a heavy rainstorm or buried by a rockslide. Cell phones are useful in emergencies, but keep in mind that they may not always be able to pick up a signal in the boondocks.

A Final Word

As you visit the places described in this guidebook, you will soon realize that Oregon's wild areas and wildlife are valuable beyond all measure. Over the years, many people have worked to protect and preserve our state's natural heritage for present and future generations of Oregonians. Be one of those people. Join a conservation organization, volunteer to clean up a river, or teach your children about the value of the natural world.

There are many ways to lend a hand. With your help, the places and wild creatures described in this guidebook will still be around long after these pages have fallen into tatters.

Legend

Interstate Highway	══🛡5══	Park/Refuge	
U.S. Highway	═26═101═	Point of Interest	◻
State Highway	══220══	Airport	✈
County Road	══21══	Camping	△
Forest Road	══220══	Parking	P
Unpaved Road	━━━━	Site Number	❸
Boundary	━ ━ ━ ━	Site/Area Locator	◯ ◻
Trail	··············	Town	◦ BURNS
Creek	∼∼∼	Peak	▲
River	∼∼∼	Spillway/Powerhouse	━━━
Lake	⬬		
Glacier	≋≋	Compass	N↑

Trip Locator Map

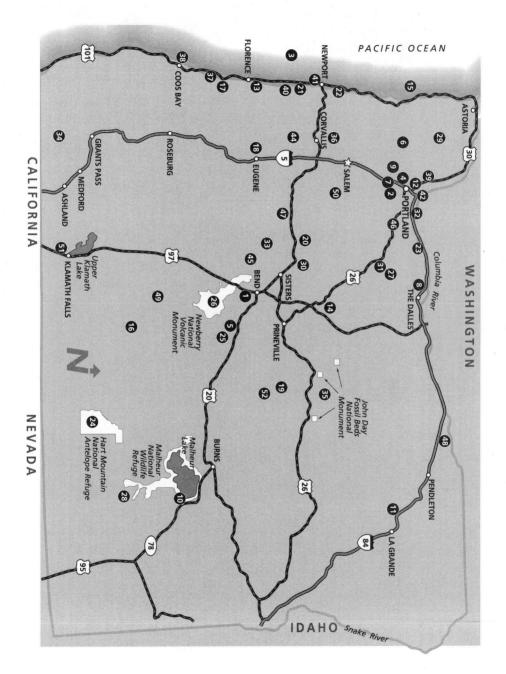

Springtime, when Oregon dons its showy wildflowers, is the ideal time to hike through Tillamook State Forest, west of Portland.

Spring

Desert on Display

This world-class museum features a host of innovative exhibits interpreting the natural and human history of the High Desert, a region that includes portions of eight western states and one Canadian province.

Site: The High Desert Museum, 3.5 miles (5 minutes) south of Bend.

Recommended time: Early March.

Minimum time commitment: 2 hours, plus driving time.

What to bring: Mostly your curiosity, but the museum grounds offer good wildlife viewing, so binoculars are useful as well as a camera for photographing captive wildlife.

Admission fee: $6.25 for adults, $5.75 for seniors age 65 or older and for youths ages 13 to 18, $3 for children ages 5 to 12, free for younger kids. Museum memberships are available for $25 for individuals and $40 for families.

Directions: From Bend, drive 3.5 miles south on U.S. Highway 97. The museum entrance is on the left (east) side of the road.

The world-class exhibits at the High Desert Museum attract visitors from all over the country.

The Rain Shadow Effect

If you have ever wondered why the Oregon desert is so dry, turn to the west and look at the snow-covered Cascade Mountains for the answer.

The Oregon desert once had a moist, tropical climate. But beginning in the Miocene Period, 5 to 24 million years ago, a great block of earth began to tilt upward, eventually forming the Cascade Range and dramatically affecting the climate in regions to the east.

This new mountain range created what is called a rain shadow. Previously, moist, warm air blew in from the Pacific Ocean, creating a warm, wet climate in what is now central and eastern Oregon. But mountains affect weather patterns. As moist air smacks up against the side of a mountain range, it begins to rise. As it rises, it cools and dumps its load of water on the western and southern slopes of the mountain range. By the time the ocean air mass reaches the eastern side of the peaks, most of its moisture is gone.

This rain shadow effect is what accounts for the considerable difference in precipitation between western and eastern Oregon. More than 100 inches may fall each year in some coastal areas, while less than 15 inches falls east of the mountains. The rain shadow cast by the Cascade Range stretches all the way into Idaho. ∎

The background: Since opening its doors in 1982, the High Desert Museum has grown from a small, local museum to a world-class educational facility interpreting the human and natural history of the arid Intermountain West. The mission of the museum is "to broaden the knowledge and understanding of the natural and cultural history and resources of the High Desert for the purpose of promoting thoughtful decision-making that will sustain the region's natural and cultural heritage." The museum hopes to accomplish this objective through a mix of traditional exhibits, outdoor exhibits, captive wildlife, live demonstrations, classes for adults and kids, annual events, field trips, and much more.

A couple of hours—or a day—at the High Desert Museum is the perfect way to get to know this fascinating region of the West and a great place to introduce kids to its natural history.

The fun: Start inside the museum with a walk through the Hall of Exploration and Settlement, a set of eight dioramas, complete with sound effects, that depict the human relationship with this desert region. Then head for the Desertarium, a series of live animal exhibits including both natural and artificially created environments. Here you will find lizards, snakes, cutthroat trout, burrowing owls, pallid bats, kangaroo rats, barn owls, and other denizens of the desert. Museum volunteers are available to answer questions, and they often have a snake, owl, or other critter with them, giving visitors the opportunity to get up close and personal.

There are 110 acres of museum grounds, including more exhibits along a paved loop trail. A favorite is the river otter exhibit, where you can peer into an otter den or watch the animals cavort underwater from an underground observatory.

Other outdoor animal exhibits include a porcupine enclosure and an ever-popular presentation on birds of prey, which is offered regularly throughout the day. Audience members are treated to a lively talk about High Desert raptors, and they meet a live cast of eagles, hawks, owls, and vultures. Other presentations focus on porcupines, otters, and occasional special subjects.

Food and lodging: All services are available in Bend. There is a small restaurant at the museum that serves soup, sandwiches, and other deli food.

Next best: From the museum, drive 9.5 miles south on US 97 to Lava Lands Visitor Center. Part of Newberry National Volcanic Monument, the visitor center has a variety of exhibits describing the fiery volcanic history of central Oregon (see trip 26).

For more information:
The High Desert Museum
59800 South Highway 97
Bend, OR 97702
541-382-4754

Great Blue Commune 2

A common bird often seen flying high in the sky, the great blue heron nests communally in the spring. One Portland-area rookery is easily visible from a park at the confluence of the Clackamas and Willamette Rivers.

Site: Clackamette Park in Oregon City, 17 miles (25 minutes) southeast of Portland.
Recommended time: Mid-March.
Minimum time commitment: 1 hour, plus driving time.

What to bring: A spotting scope is best, but binoculars will work.

Admission fee: None.

Directions: From Interstate 5, 8 miles south of Portland, take exit 288 and head east on Interstate 205. Drive 8.7 miles to exit 9 for Oregon City and Gladstone. Turn north onto Oregon Highway 99E and drive 0.2 mile. Turn left at the light. There is a sign for Clackamette Park at this intersection. Following signs to the park, turn right onto Clackamette Drive and go 0.2 mile. Turn left into the park. Make an immediate left onto a gravel road before entering the main parking lot, and follow the road around to where the Clackamas River flows into the Willamette River. Park there.

The background: Great blue herons are a common bird of the Pacific Northwest, even in urban areas. Often seen flying overhead, these birds travel long distances each day to use a variety of habitats, although they are most commonly found in wetland areas.

Elegant, long-legged, fish-eating birds, great blue herons were hunted early in this century for their feathers, which were used to decorate ladies' hats. Today, the species is nearly ubiquitous in Oregon, and it uses virtually any type of habitat found here except desert and deep forest.

Great blue herons gather in colonies during the early spring to build bulky nests of sticks, typically high in large trees. These nesting colonies are called rookeries. The females begin laying eggs in March and April. The young birds hatch in about a month and fledge by September.

From Clackamette Park, you can see a great blue heron rookery on Goat Island in the Willamette River.

The fun: Park on the gravel road that runs along the river at the westernmost point of the park, and walk the short distance through berry brambles to where the Clackamas River flows into the Willamette River. Goat Island is directly west of this point.

Look high in the trees on the island for the bulky nests as well as for birds in their nests, perching on branches, and flying back and forth from the river to the island.

Food and lodging: All services are available in Oregon City.

Next best: There are other great blue heron rookeries in the Portland metropolitan area, some of which are more sensitive to human disturbance. Some are accessible only by boat. The Portland Audubon Society offers tours to local rookeries as part of its Great Blue Heron Week activities in May. Call the society at 503-292-6855 for more information.

For more information:

Oregon Department of Fish and Wildlife

17330 SE Evelyn Street

Clackamas, OR 97015

503-657-2000

Thar She Blows 3

Gray whales migrate along the Oregon Coast between their summer and fall feeding grounds in the Bering Sea and calving area along the coast of Mexico. You can see them, often very close to shore, from many vantage points along the coast.

Site: Various headlands along the coast.

Recommended time: Mid- to late March.

Minimum time commitment: 1 day.

What to bring: Rain gear, warm coat, binoculars.

Admission fee: None.

Directions: There are many good places along the coast to watch whales. All you need is a good, elevated view of the surrounding ocean and sharp eyes. Some of the more popular whale-watching locations are Tillamook Head, Cape Falcon, Cape Meares, Cape Lookout, Cascade Head, Cape Foulweather, Yaquina Head, Cape Perpetua, Heceta Head, Cape Arago, Cape Blanco, and Cape Sebastian.

The background: Gray whales travel a 10,000-mile migration circuit each year, passing the Oregon coast during March and April as they journey north to their summer and fall feeding grounds in the Bering Sea. During good weather, these 35-ton marine mammals can be seen within a few hundred yards of shore. During peak migration periods, as many as 30 whales may pass by each hour.

During the migration of the gray whales, the Oregon Parks and Recreation Department sponsors a whale-watching program called "Whale Watching Spoken Here." Volunteers are stationed at about 30 locations along the coast during the Christmas and spring school holidays, collecting data on the number of whales passing by, helping members of the public spot whales, and providing information about the natural history of these impressive animals.

The fun: Any location along the coast with an expansive view of the ocean can make a good whale-watching location. It is easier to spot whales during the morning, when the sun is behind you. The best approach is to scan the water with your naked eye, watching for spouts. When you spot a whale "blowing," switch to binoculars for a close-up look.

Usually, you will see just the backs and tails of the 45-foot-long animals as they come up for air and then dive. On warmer days, the whales seem to

Coastal Headlands

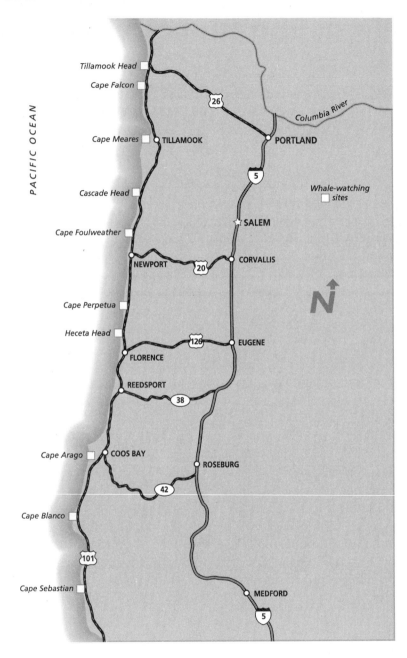

PACIFIC OCEAN

Tillamook Head
Cape Falcon

26
Columbia River

Cape Meares   TILLAMOOK
PORTLAND

5

Cascade Head
Whale-watching
sites

Cape Foulweather
SALEM

NEWPORT   20   CORVALLIS

N

Cape Perpetua

Heceta Head
126   EUGENE
FLORENCE

REEDSPORT
38

Cape Arago   COOS BAY
ROSEBURG

42

Cape Blanco

101

Cape Sebastian
MEDFORD

5

A Whale's Tale

Traveling 10,000 miles round-trip each year between the warm waters off Mexico and the frigid waters off Alaska, the 35-ton gray whale is one of the earth's greatest long-distance migrants.

Gray whales are baleen whales, which means they have "fringed" plates instead of teeth which they use to filter shrimplike animals, called amphipods, off the ocean floor and into their mouths. The whales lick these tasty morsels off their baleen filter with their tongues.

The whales spend mid-spring through mid-fall feeding in the Chukchi and Bering Seas off the coast of Alaska. Then, as winter approaches, the whales begin their southern migration, passing the coast of the Pacific Northwest between December and mid-February. During their migration, they swim at a rate of about 5 miles per hour, reaching their breeding grounds in lagoons off the Mexican coast in about three weeks. During this time, the whales eat little or nothing for up to five months.

Gray whale calves are born between late December and early February. They are about 15 feet long and weigh around 1 ton at birth. The calves nurse for six to eight months.

Whales pass the Oregon coast on their northern migration between March and April. Adult males and females without calves leave the breeding grounds first, followed by females with young.

The gray whale's 10,000-mile odyssey is the longest migration undertaken by any mammal. Scientists studying whales believe that they may navigate by swimming close to shore and listening to the sound of the surf, which tells them which side the shore is on and therefore which way they are heading.

Gray whales were a prime target for 19th-century whalers, and their population was so severely reduced by the early 1900s that the Mexican government closed the gray whaling industry off its coast. In 1937, the League of Nations gave gray whales full protection from whaling. The International Whaling Commission followed suit in 1946. This protection has helped the gray whale population rebound. Over 20,000 of the great mammals are believed to be plying the North Pacific today—about the same number that existed prior to the whaling period. In 1994, the gray whale was removed from the federal government's list of endangered species. ■

spend more time near the surface. If you are lucky, you may see them poking their heads straight out of the water (called "spy-hopping") to have a look around. Or you may see them "breaching," which is when a whale lifts up to three-quarters of its body length out of the water and then crashes back down with a great splash.

Food and lodging: All services are available in most coastal communities.

Next best: Whales also pass along the coast on their southern migration to calving grounds in the warm waters off the coast of Mexico. The first weekend in January is usually the peak viewing time for this migration.

For more information:

Whale Watching Spoken Here

Oregon Parks and Recreation Department

P.O. Box 693

Waldport, OR 97394

541-563-2002

A Trillion Trilliums 4

Spring has returned to western Oregon when the trillium, one of the earliest flowers to bloom, unfolds its delicate white-to-pink petals at Tryon Creek State Natural Area.

Site: Tryon Creek State Natural Area, 2.3 miles (10 minutes) off Interstate 5 in southwest Portland.

Recommended time: Late March or early April.

Minimum time commitment: 3 hours, plus driving time.

What to bring: Rain gear (the weather is often nice during early spring, but just in case), hiking boots, camera with close-up lens, field guide to wildflowers.

Admission fee: None.

Directions: In Portland, take exit 297 off I-5. Go right on Southwest Terwilliger Boulevard and drive 2.3 miles, bearing left where the road intersects with Southwest Boones Ferry Road and passing the Lewis and Clark Northwestern School of Law. Turn right (west) into the park at the sign. Drive the short distance to the parking area and visitor center.

The background: A flower of moist, shady, low-elevation forests, the trillium may bloom as early as February in some years, making it a sure harbinger of spring in western Oregon. In Tryon Creek State Natural Area, it is usu-

Celebrate the first wildflowers of spring with a March hike through trillium-strewn Tryon Creek State Natural Area in Portland.

ally at its peak from mid-March through early April.

This forested 645-acre park, managed by the Oregon Parks and Recreation Department, is the perfect place to greet the first trilliums of the spring. The park features 8 miles of hiking trails, equestrian trails, bicycle paths, a nature center, and a variety of public educational programs.

On the first weekend in April, the Friends of Tryon Creek State Park sponsor the Trillium Festival, which features guided walks to see wildflowers (including trilliums), food booths, local craft vendors, and a native plant sale for gardeners who want to add a little wildness to their garden. The event is a fundraiser for the Friends of Tryon Creek State Park, and the proceeds are used for educational programs, park maintenance, and similar endeavors that benefit the natural area and visitors. When Easter falls on the first weekend in April, the festival is held on the last weekend in March. Either way, the event coincides with the peak trillium blooming period.

The fun: Attend the Trillium Festival and take a free guided nature walk to see the flowers and learn about the ecology of the surrounding Douglas-fir forest. If you want to go it on your own, virtually any trail in the park leads to trilliums at this time of year. For a short, easy walk, take the 0.35-mile Trillium Trail, which begins just south of the nature center. It is paved and barrier free. The 1.2-mile Middle Creek Loop, which also begins at the nature center, takes you into the canyon, along Tryon Creek, and back to your starting point. There is a total of 14 interconnecting hiking trails through the natural area.

Food and lodging: All services are available throughout the Portland area.

Next best: Volunteers from the Friends of Tryon Creek State Park lead guided nature walks in the natural area every Saturday and Sunday throughout June, July, and August.

For more information:

Tryon Creek State Natural Area
Oregon Parks and Recreation Department
11321 SW Terwilliger Boulevard
Portland, OR 97219
503-636-9886

Dance of
the Sage Grouse   5

In the early morning hours each spring, male sage grouse gather at this traditional mating ground to strut and posture in an effort to attract a mate.

Site: Millican Lekking Site, 20 miles (30 minutes) east of Bend.

Recommended time: Early April.

Minimum time commitment: 4 hours, plus driving time.

What to bring: Warm clothes, hot drinks, snacks, binoculars, spotting scope, camera with telephoto lens.

Admission fee: None.

Directions: Take U.S. Highway 20 east from Bend for 17.4 miles and turn right onto Evans Well Road (it is not signed, but it is the first right at the bottom of the grade). Drive 1.1 miles, turn right onto a dirt road, and go 0.25 mile to the parking area.

The background: Sage grouse gather at this open area in the sagebrush plains outside Bend each spring to perform their courtship and mating rituals. Males puff out their wings, spread their tail feathers, and inflate colorful air sacs on their necks while performing a ritualized dance designed to attract a mate and scare off other suitors. The mating displays begin at dawn and usually last until mid-morning. After mating, the females leave the area to build a nest, lay and incubate eggs, and raise the chicks. These traditional nesting locations, called leks, are used year after year.

The fun: Plan to arrive just before dawn, because mating activity will begin shortly thereafter. You can situate your vehicle in the parking area so that you can see the lekking area just to the north from the car. The sage grouse tend to be about 100 yards off and are easily visible with binoculars or a spotting scope.

Depending on current population levels, up to 100 sage grouse may gather here. The males arrive first and often begin their display ritual before the hens show up. You will see them fluff out their feathers, gulp air to inflate their air sacs, rub their wings against their breasts, repeatedly run forward a short distance, and then make popping sounds by bouncing their air sacs up and down. This display is repeated by each bird up to five times an hour. When the hens, waiting nearby, decide they are ready to mate, they come forward and select a male. After breeding, the hens depart for the sagebrush to nest.

Although the sage grouse here are fairly tolerant of people, it is best if you stay in your vehicle while watching. This site is open to the public only during the month of April. Staff members from the Bureau of Land Management are here on weekends to answer questions about sage grouse.

Food and lodging: All services are available in Bend.

Next best: Mating activity goes on through April, but fewer birds are present toward the end of the breeding period, when only males may remain at the lek.

For more information:

Bureau of Land Management
3050 NE Third Street
Prineville, OR 97754
541-416-6700

In the Fire's Wake 6

A springtime walk in Tillamook State Forest, which was devastated by wildfire in the 1930s and 1940s, dramatically showcases the healing powers of nature.

Site: Gales Creek Trail, Tillamook State Forest, about 42 miles (1 hour) west of Portland.

The dense foliage of Tillamook State Forest makes it hard to believe that this area was once seemingly destroyed by wildfire.

Recommended time: Mid-April.

Minimum time commitment: 2 hours, plus driving time.

What to bring: Clothing appropriate for the weather, sturdy hiking boots, trail snacks, water, camera.

Admission fee: None.

Directions: Drive west from Portland on U.S. Highway 26 about 24 miles to the junction with Oregon Highway 6. Turn west onto OR 6 and drive 18.3 miles to the Gales Creek Trailhead on the right (north) side of the road.

The background: On August 14, 1933, a hot and windy day, a fire started at a logging operation in Gales Creek Canyon. The woods were so dry that in minutes the fire was racing through the forest. Ten days later, despite the efforts of a thousand firefighters, the fire had burned 240,000 acres of the Coast Range in northwestern Oregon, sending plumes of smoke 40,000 feet into the sky. It was one of the largest forest fires in the modern history of the United States. From 1933 to 1951, forest fires struck the area at six-year intervals, eventually claiming 355,000 acres of forest. These conflagrations came to be known collectively as the Tillamook Burn.

Over that 18-year period, those fires destroyed nearly 13.2 billion board feet of timber valued at $7 billion, profoundly affecting the area's economy. The impact of the fires on the environment was equally serious. Wildlife habitat was destroyed, and rivers were filled with debris and sediment.

In 1948, Oregon voters passed a bond measure to finance the replanting of the Tillamook Burn. Beginning in 1940, the Oregon Board of Forestry began to acquire lands within the Tillamook Burn, forming what would eventually become, in 1973, the 364,000-acre Tillamook State Forest.

Between 1948 and 1973, 72 million Douglas-fir seedlings were planted in the Tillamook Burn and 72,000 pounds of Douglas-fir seeds were dropped from aircraft to help the forest recover. Today, the dense growth of trees within the Tillamook State Forest makes it hard to picture the fiery devastation that once existed here.

The fun: The 2-mile Gales Creek Trail descends 632 feet to Gales Creek Campground through a regrown forest of Douglas-fir. It was this part of the forest that was destroyed in the original 1933 Tillamook Burn. Today, the undergrowth is lush as the trail follows an old railroad grade and then skirts the east bank of the West Fork of Gales Creek before passing through a meadow of cottonwoods, red alders, and vine maples. As the trail nears the campground, it rejoins the old railroad bed, which was formerly used to haul freshly cut logs out of the forest by train.

You can also begin this hike at Gales Creek Campground, which is off OR 6,

Forest Fire: Friend or Foe?

Wildfire has long played a role in the ecology of forests. Fires that started naturally, usually by lightning, swept through the forests of the West on a regular basis. As a result, forest ecosystems and the species found there have adapted to fire.

In the eastern portions of Oregon, low-intensity fires periodically passed through forests of ponderosa pine, fir, and larch, burning undergrowth and accumulations of needles, cones, and other detritus. The result was an open parklike environment.

Fires were less frequent in the Douglas-fir region of western Oregon. When they happened, usually during periods of prolonged drought, they often burned with great intensity due to the large amounts of logs, limbs, and other combustible material on the forest floor typical of this area.

But the openings in the forest that the fires created were soon colonized by a variety of species of plants and trees that needed lots of sun to thrive. This new growth in turn provided food and habitat for wildlife species, such as deer, that preferred the open, brushy areas to deep forest. This mix of mature forest and burned-over areas in various stages of regrowth resulted in a mosaic of plant and tree species that increased the overall diversity of the landscape.

Although the native peoples inhabiting the Northwest forests sometimes set fires to stimulate the regrowth of berries and other plants, the arrival of white settlers to the area marked a change in attitudes about forest fires. To protect property and valuable timber, an aggressive program of extinguishing forest fires was put into place.

While firefighters have saved many lives, homes, and trees from flames over the years, the long-term environmental effects have recently begun to crop up. For example, in the Blue Mountains of northeastern Oregon, years of fire suppression have allowed large amounts of undergrowth to accumulate, increasing the risk that future fires may burn so hot that they will be impossible to put out and will do far more damage to the forest than past fires have. Eliminating fire has also allowed for more growth of fir trees—a species usually burned off by the natural fire cycle—and these have crowded out the pines and larches, making the forests more vulnerable to diseases and insect attacks.

Today, foresters recognize the value of fire as part of the forest ecosystem and are working to integrate it into their management plans. This includes letting nature-caused fires run their course in wilderness areas and using controlled burns to reduce the accumulation of combustible detritus on the forest floor. ■

about 2.5 miles east of the roadside (or Summit) trailhead. The hike from this direction is uphill and a bit more strenuous.

Food and lodging: All (and nearest) services are available in Tillamook, 32 miles west on OR 6.

Next best: There are seven hiking trails in Tillamook State Forest that are accessible from OR 6. They range in length from 2 to 9 miles. A map and brochure are available from the Oregon Department of Forestry office in Tillamook.

For more information:

Tillamook State Forest
Oregon Department of Forestry
4907 East Third Street
Tillamook, OR 97141
503-842-2545

A Cacophony of Camas

7

Camas in hues of deep purple bloom in profusion at this urban nature preserve.

Site: Camassia, in West Linn, about 8 miles (15 minutes) south of downtown Portland.

Recommended time: Late April.

Minimum time commitment: 2 hours, plus driving time.

What to bring: Camera with close-up lens, magnifying glass (for examining flowers), flower identification guide, binoculars, waterproof hiking boots.

Admission fee: None.

Directions: From Interstate 5, 8 miles south of downtown Portland, take exit 288 and head east on Interstate 205 for 8.2 miles to exit 8 in West Linn. Go right at the stoplight at the bottom of the exit, drive 0.5 mile, and turn right onto Willamette Falls Drive (just before the BP gas station). Travel 0.3 mile and turn right onto Sunset Avenue. Go 0.2 mile and turn right onto Walnut Street. Drive to the end of the road and the small parking area. The trail begins here.

The background: Camassia is a 26-acre nature preserve owned by the Nature Conservancy and named after the abundance of camas that grows there. Although not uncommon, camas is a quintessential and strikingly beautiful flower of the Pacific Northwest. Its bulb was gathered and eaten by Native Americans as well as by early pioneers. A mix of grassy plateaus, oak woodlands, wet meadows, and some swales of aspens and willows characterizes this small piece of native habitat surrounded by the hustle and bustle of city life.

Over 300 species of plants grow on the preserve. A variety of bird species, including towhees, bushtits, robins, hairy woodpeckers, and California quail, find habitat here as well. Floods exposed the basalt outcroppings here 12,000 to 19,000 years ago.

The fun: An interpretive signboard at the trailhead has a map of the preserve and its trails. The best places to see camas and other wildflowers are on the grassy plateaus and in the oak–madrone woodlands. The right-hand trail leads from the trailhead to the East Plateau. It will take only a few minutes to reach the plateau through dense forest. In these open areas, the camas is easy to spot.

Camas blooms in abundance at Camassia, in the heart of the Portland metropolitan area.

Preserve trails are narrow and may be wet and muddy, although there are some short boardwalks over the wetter trail segments. You will also encounter wet and swampy areas on the plateaus. Poison oak grows on the preserve, so be aware of what it looks like (see page 28).

Although Camassia is open to the public, it is owned by a private organization. Please respect the area, keep to the trails, do not pick the flowers, and

Camassia

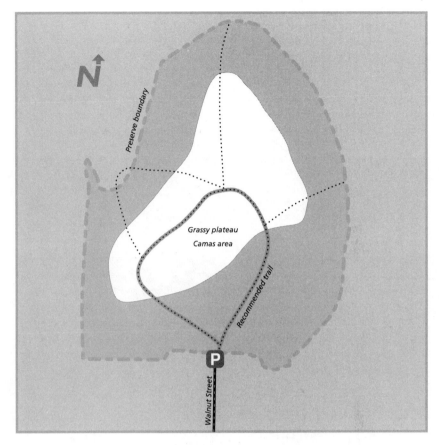

leave your dog at home. The Nature Conservancy staff also asks that groups of 10 or more planning to visit here call their office first.

Food and lodging: All services are available in West Linn and nearby Portland.

Next best: The show of camas is best from April through early May, but you will still find some blooming for a couple of weeks after the peak.

For more information:

The Nature Conservancy of Oregon
821 SE 14th Avenue
Portland, OR 97214
503-230-1221

Attack of the Alien Vegetation

Mixed in with the palette of colorful native wildflowers that grow in fields, along roadsides, on rangeland, and across the Oregon landscape are alien invaders that, to the untrained eye, are as pretty as any other Oregon wildflower.

But beauty is in the eye of the beholder. These invaders are nonnative plants that, over many years, have established themselves in various habitats throughout the state, often with dire consequences for native plants.

From the showy dalmation toadflax to the nondescript hoary cress, a host of plants from other countries—the Mediterranean and Eurasia in particular—has immigrated to the United States over the years, often when grain and crop seed shipments were contaminated with the plants' seeds. Once here, the seeds spread from place to place by getting mixed in with hay shipped to ranchers for cattle feed, tucked inside the coats of sheep and other livestock, and even stuck on the treads of car tires and shoe soles.

Once established, these alien plants can overwhelm and wipe out native plant populations. Many of them are noxious weeds that provide little food value for wildlife and livestock and may even be poisonous.

A case in point is the yellow star thistle. This plant, which grows up to 3 feet tall and sports colorful yellow flowers, was first detected in California in the early 1800s, when seeds were found mixed into adobe used to make bricks. Barely 100 years later, the plant began to show up in the Pacific Northwest. Today, about 150,000 acres of rangeland in Oregon, along with a similar amount in Washington, 300,000 acres in Idaho, and 10 million acres in California, are infested with yellow star thistle. Each plant is capable of producing up to 150,000 seeds, so it is not hard to see how it spread so quickly and extensively. Toxic to horses, this invasive weed can completely overwhelm native grasses, which are invaluable forage for both wildlife and livestock.

Land managers, scientists, and conservationists are battling the spread of nonnative plants using everything in their arsenal, from spraying with herbicides to getting on their hands and knees and pulling them from the ground one by one. But many noxious weeds are so entrenched that we will probably never be entirely rid of them. In these cases, probably the best we can hope for is to slow their spread. ■

8

Bloom with a View

Native wildflowers bloom in profusion on the expansive Rowena Plateau, overlooking the mighty Columbia River.

Site: Tom McCall Preserve at Rowena, 70 miles (1.5 hours) east of Portland.

Recommended time: Late April.

Minimum time commitment: 3 hours, plus driving time.

What to bring: Windbreaker (it is often very windy on the plateau), hiking boots, water, lunch or snacks, camera with close-up and wide-angle lenses, flower identification guide.

Admission fee: None, but there is a drop box at the trailhead for donations.

Directions: From Portland, drive east on Interstate 84 for 64 miles to the Mosier exit (exit 69). Go right at the bottom of the exit onto Oregon Highway 30. Follow OR 30 for 6.5 miles. This is part of the Columbia River Gorge scenic highway, and much of it is steep and winding. The trailhead is on the left. Almost directly across the road is the Rowena Viewpoint, which offers expansive views of the Columbia River to the east.

More than 300 native species of plants grow at Tom McCall Preserve, within view of the mighty Columbia River.

The background: Purchased in parcels between 1978 and 1993 by the Nature Conservancy, this preserve is named after Oregon's renowned governor Tom McCall who, during the early 1970s, helped develop Oregon's pioneering land-use laws, which have been instrumental in maintaining the state's well-known quality of life.

This 231-acre piece of real estate on Rowena Plateau overlooking the Columbia River is a refuge for such native plants as shooting stars, arrowleaf balsamroot, paintbrush, and lupine, as well as native grasses. Over 300 native plant species grow here, including Columbia desert parsley, Hood River milkvetch, Thompson's broadleaf lupine, and Thompson's waterleaf, all of which are unique to the Columbia River Gorge area.

The Nature Conservancy monitors the various plant species on the preserve and works to control nonnative noxious weeds as part of its management program. It also offers interpretive hikes here during spring and summer.

The fun: Park at the small trailhead at the preserve entrance, where an interpretive sign will introduce you to the area. The 1-mile plateau trail begins here and leads across open, flower-filled grasslands with breathtaking views of the Columbia River, as well as into side canyons and around a prairie pond. There are rattlesnakes and poison oak on the preserve, so be aware.

Although Tom McCall Preserve is open to the public, it is owned by a private organization. Please respect the area, keep to the trails, do not pick the flowers, and leave your dog at home. The Nature Conservancy staff also asks that groups of 10 or more planning to visit the preserve call the conservancy office.

Food and lodging: All services are available in Hood River, 11 miles to the west along I-84.

Next best: If you are not able to make it during the February-to-June flower-blooming season, go anyway. With its grasslands and Columbia River vistas, Tom McCall Preserve is one of the loveliest spots in Oregon.

For more information:

The Nature Conservancy of Oregon
821 SE 14th Avenue
Portland, OR 97214
503-230-1221

Poison Oak

Spring Has Sprung 9

Spring is a busy time at Jackson Bottom Wetlands Preserve as migrating birds arrive to nest, frogs call in the night for mates, and wildlife seems to shake off the rainy winter doldrums as eagerly as humans.

Site: Jackson Bottom Wetlands Preserve, Hillsboro, 25 miles (40 minutes) west of Portland.

Recommended time: Early May.

Minimum time commitment: 2 hours, plus driving time.

What to bring: Binoculars or spotting scope, camera and telephoto lens, bird identification guide.

Admission fee: None.

Directions: From Portland, drive west on U.S. Highway 26 for about 20 miles. Take the North Plains/Hillsboro exit. Turn left onto Glencoe Road and go 5 miles to Hillsboro, where Glencoe Road becomes South First Avenue. Continue over the railroad tracks where the road becomes Oregon Highway 219. The North View Site, which has a viewing platform, is on the left 0.6 mile south of Hillsboro. The South View Site and trailhead is 0.8 mile beyond the North View Site, on the left.

The background: Located within the city limits of Hillsboro in the Tualatin River basin, this 650-acre preserve is composed primarily of wetland. There are five streams in the area, woodlands on higher ground, and former farmland that has reverted to natural meadows.

This city-owned marshland serves a number of purposes, which include providing habitat for wildlife and a venue in which to educate the public about the environment. But the most intriguing purpose is its function as a component of the city sewage-treatment facility, naturally "polishing" wastewater and rendering it clean enough to release into the nearby Tualatin River. To accomplish this feat, the city fills ponds in the preserve and irrigates fields with wastewater previously treated at its wastewater treatment plant. Over time, the soil and plants of the wetland leach out nitrogen, phosphorous, chemical waste, and excess sediments, which can have harmful effects on rivers and streams.

While these details are of no concern to the preserve's wildlife, the benefits of the wetlands are not lost on them. A host of wildlife inhabits the area,

Pacific tree frogs are common residents of Jackson Bottom Wetlands Preserve.

including ducks, geese, great blue herons, and other water-loving birds; a variety of songbirds; deer; otters; beavers; and amphibians such as the Pacific tree frog.

The fun: Park at the South View Site and hike the 2-mile Kingfisher Marsh Trail, which runs along the Tualatin River and through Kingfisher Marsh, an artificial marsh created in 1990. The trail passes two wildlife-viewing blinds and a river viewpoint as it winds its way through the preserve. Watch for waterfowl and great blue herons at the retention pond and Kingfisher Marsh, and watch for songbirds in the vegetation along the river. The blinds provide you with views of the retention pond and Kingfisher Marsh.

The trail begins at the southwestern corner of the parking area, where there is a sign with a map of the preserve. For an expansive view of the southern half of the marshland, walk a short distance up the trail on the southeastern side of the parking lot, bearing left at the intersection. The covered viewing platform here is a good place to scan the wetlands with binoculars or a spotting scope. The trail is open daily from dawn to dusk.

Although there is no trail access, you will have a good view of the northern part of the preserve from the viewing platform at the North View Site, 0.8 mile north of the South View Site off OR 219 on the east side of the road.

Mornings and evenings are the best times to see and hear wildlife at the preserve.

Food and lodging: All services are available in Hillsboro.

Next best: Winter is also an excellent time to visit the preserve to see migrating waterfowl.

For more information:
Jackson Bottom Wetlands Preserve
City of Hillsboro
123 West Main Street
Hillsboro, OR 97123
503-681-6206

Desert Oasis

10

See migrating and nesting birds galore at one of the country's top national wildlife refuges.

Site: Malheur National Wildlife Refuge, 36 miles (45 minutes) south of Burns.

Recommended time: Mid-May.

Minimum time commitment: 1 to 2 days.

What to bring: Binoculars or spotting scope, bird identification guide, camera with telephoto lens, insect repellent. At this time of year, the desert is characterized by cold mornings and nights and pleasant sunny days, although bad weather is not unheard of. Bring clothing appropriate for a wide range of temperatures and weather conditions.

Admission fee: None.

Directions: From Burns, go east on Oregon Highway 78 for 2 miles and then south on OR 205 for 25 miles. Turn left (east) onto Narrows–Princeton Road and go 9 miles to the refuge headquarters.

The background: This 185,000-acre national wildlife refuge in the heart of the Great Basin Desert is regarded as one of the best birding hot spots in the nation. Ponds, lakes, marshlands, meadows, and rangelands combine to provide habitat for a variety of wildlife.

About 300 species of birds have been documented at the refuge. Birds likely to be encountered on a springtime trip here include a wide variety of waterfowl and shorebirds, such as egrets, tundra swans, and sandhill cranes. Hawks, owls, red-winged blackbirds, warblers, and a multitude of other species are found here as well. Mule deer, pronghorn antelope, coyotes, and jackrabbits are also commonly seen.

Hiking is limited on the refuge during the spring and summer to protect

Malheur National Wildlife Refuge

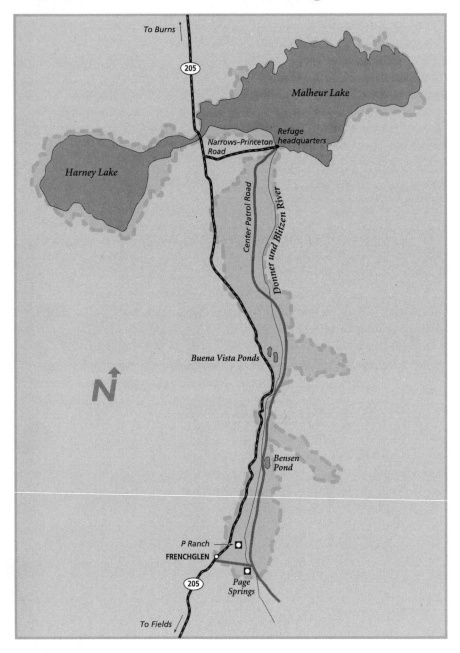

To Burns

205

Malheur Lake

Refuge headquarters

Narrows–Princeton Road

Harney Lake

Center Patrol Road

Donner und Blitzen River

Buena Vista Ponds

N

Bensen Pond

P Ranch

FRENCHGLEN

205

Page Springs

To Fields

Malheur National Wildlife Refuge, an oasis in the heart of the Great Basin Desert, is one of the nation's renowned birding areas.

nesting birds. But the Center Patrol Road, which runs through the center of the refuge along the Donner und Blitzen River, provides plenty of opportunities for viewing wildlife from your car. In fact, it is recommended that you stay in your vehicle because you will be less likely to frighten wildlife away.

A highlight of the refuge is the headquarters, which offers a museum, bookstore, and pleasant grounds with lots of shade trees—a great place for a picnic.

The fun: If you have at least a full day, start out at the refuge headquarters, wander through the museum and bookstore, and get the locations of the latest and most interesting wildlife sightings from refuge staff. Then drive the Center Patrol Road south through the refuge for about 53 miles to Page Springs, near Frenchglen, watching for wildlife as you go. The P Ranch and Page Springs areas are especially good places to see songbirds in the spring. Benson Pond and Buena Vista Ponds are excellent places to observe water birds.

Food and lodging: All services are available in Burns. In Frenchglen, rooms are available at the Frenchglen Hotel, but advanced reservations are advised. There is also a restaurant in town. Public and commercial campgrounds are available just outside Frenchglen.

Next best: Those on a tight schedule will want to visit just the refuge headquarters and then head south on OR 205 to the Diamond Lane turnoff to

Vanishing Wetlands

While many people think of swamps when they hear the word *wetland*, freshwater wetlands actually encompass a variety of watery habitats, including marshes, rivers and streams, ponds and lakes, and woodland bogs. Each habitat is a bit different, as are the kinds of animals that live there.

In Oregon, marshes are characteristic of wetland areas east of the Cascade Mountains and are often the remnants of once-large lakes created by melting glaciers at the end of the last ice age, 10,000 to 15,000 years ago. Cattails and bulrushes are typical plants of these oases in the desert. Marshes that lie along the Pacific Flyway, the migration route for West Coast waterfowl, are important resting and feeding areas for migratory ducks, geese, and other water birds. For example, up to 250,000 ducks may use Malheur National Wildlife Refuge during migration periods.

Dense stands of willows, alders, and other trees and shrubs growing along streams and rivers provide nesting habitat for songbirds. Beavers also like to make their homes in woodland wetlands, where there are plenty of trees for food and plenty of water to provide safety from predators. Frogs and salamanders rely on marshes and other water-rich habitats to breed and lay eggs. Over a dozen species of waterfowl nest in wetland areas, as well as many other kinds of birds. Other wetland dwellers include muskrats, mink, and otters.

In addition to the important habitat they provide for wildlife, wetlands act as a natural filtration system, straining out sediments, pollutants, and other impurities as water flows through the marsh environment.

But America's wetlands are vanishing, mostly because they are being drained to make way for human development. In the 1780s, there were an estimated 221 million acres of wetlands in the lower 48 states. By the 1980s, there was only about 104 million acres. Oregon alone has lost nearly 40 percent of its original wetlands. ∎

drive the southern half of the Center Patrol Road, which tends to feature the best wildlife viewing.

For more information:

Malheur National Wildlife Refuge
HC 72, Box 245
Princeton, OR 97721
541-493-2612

Owl Watching Is a Hoot

Here are good opportunities to see relatively rare and reclusive great gray owls from mid-May to early June as the young fledge from their nests and parent birds hunt for prey to feed them.

Site: Spring Creek Great Gray Owl Management Area, 15 miles (25 minutes) west of La Grande, 40 miles (1 hour) southeast of Pendleton.

Recommended time: Late May.

Minimum time commitment: 4 hours, plus driving time.

What to bring: Binoculars, bird identification guide, camera with telephoto lens, flashlight.

Admission fee: None.

Directions: From La Grande, drive northwest on Interstate 84 West for 13.2 miles. Exit the highway at Spring Creek Road (exit 248). Turn left (south) onto Spring Creek Road, which turns to gravel just under the overpass and becomes Forest Road 21. Go 2.7 miles to FR 700 and turn right (west). You will find places to park about 0.3 mile up the road.

The background: About eight pairs of great gray owls have nested each year in this 4-square-mile corner of the Blue Mountains since at least the early 1980s, when they were first discovered. Because great gray owls are relatively uncommon, and because this is a rather high-density nesting population, the Forest Service manages this portion of the Wallowa–Whitman National Forest for the benefit of these birds.

Great gray owls typically hunt in open forest areas and nest in snags in old-growth forests and in nests abandoned by northern goshawks. But many of the old goshawk nests here have fallen apart, and the area was logged in the 1970s, limiting the number of nesting trees available. To help the owls, the Forest Service has placed nesting platforms throughout the area—and the owls have readily used them.

Great gray owls mate in February and begin incubating their eggs from mid-March to early April. The owl chicks hatch in about a month and leave the nest when they are around four weeks old. After fledging, they stay near the nest site, being fed by their parents, for another two or three weeks. Then they set off on their own. It is at this time that you are most likely to see them in the Spring Creek area.

Spring Creek Great Gray Owl Management Area

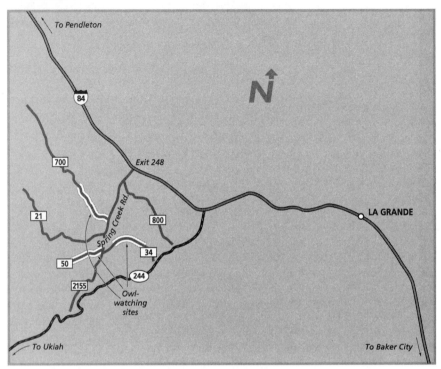

To Pendleton

N

84

700   Exit 248

LA GRANDE

21

Spring Creek Rd

800

50   34

2155   244

Owl-
watching
sites

To Ukiah   To Baker City

The fun: Great gray owls are a species of owl that regularly hunts during daylight hours. The best time to look for them is early evening. Park on FR 700, within the area marked as old-growth forest (there are signs on some of the trees), and listen for adult and juvenile birds calling and hooting to one another. Also, watch for hunting adults flying through the forest. There are nest platforms in the area that may have owls in or around them. The owls are most likely to be found within 0.25 to 1 mile of the road, so you will need to do a little walking.

Because you will be owl watching toward evening, with night coming on, be sure to keep track of the time and note how long it will take you to get back to your vehicle. The forest can be disorienting and hazardous to walk through at night, so you will want to be on your way home by dark.

Nesting activity in different parts of the Spring Creek Great Gray Owl Management Area can change from year to year. You can call the phone number listed below in April for up-to-date information on the most active nesting areas. You can also request a very helpful brochure called "Spring Creek Great Gray Owl Management Area."

Food and lodging: All services are available in La Grande and Pendleton.

Next best: The open forests off FR 50 and FR 34 are also likely spots to watch for adult great gray owls hunting. To reach FR 50, go 0.6 mile past FR 700, bear left onto FR 2155, and go 1 mile. FR 50 will be on your right. To get to FR 34, continue past FR 50 for 0.3 mile. FR 34 will be on your left.

For more information:

Wallowa-Whitman National Forest
La Grande Ranger District
3502 Highway 30
La Grande, OR 97850
541-963-7186

Salamander Central

Rough-skinned newts, one of Oregon's most abundant salamanders, trek out of the surrounding forest beginning in March as they make a beeline for the Audubon Society of Portland bird sanctuary pond, where they will breed. By mid-May, the pond is full of newts.

Site: Audubon Society of Portland Bird Sanctuary, 3 miles (10 minutes) west of downtown Portland.

Recommended time: Late May.

Minimum time commitment: 1 hour, plus driving time.

What to bring: Binoculars, camera with telephoto lens, field guides to birds and amphibians.

Admission fee: None.

Directions: From downtown Portland, follow Northwest Lovejoy Street west for about 0.6 mile until it bears to the right and becomes Northwest Cornell Road. Continue on Northwest Cornell Road for about 2 miles and through two tunnels to the Audubon sanctuary. It is on the right, 0.5 mile past the second tunnel.

The background: Found throughout western Oregon, rough-skinned newts remain hidden under logs and rocks throughout the summer. But as the fall and winter rains arrive, the newts begin to wander across the moist forest floor, often in large numbers, as they migrate to ponds and other shallow, slow-moving bodies of water to lay their eggs on aquatic vegetation during the December-to-July breeding season.

The pond at the Audubon Society of Portland's bird sanctuary is a magnet for rough-skinned newts, which migrate there in the spring to breed.

Rough-skinned newts dine on slugs, snails, insect larvae, and earthworms. They commonly live to the age of 12, but some have lived up to 26 years. Their skin secretes a toxin identical to the one secreted by puffer fish (including the Japanese culinary delicacy the fungu fish), which protects them from predators and is potentially fatal to humans. It is fine to handle the newts, but you should wash your hands afterward and keep them away from food and eating utensils.

One of the easiest places to see a gathering of rough-skinned newts is in the pond at the Audubon Society bird sanctuary, where they begin gathering in March. The sanctuary is actually three sanctuaries: the 20-acre Pittock Sanctuary and the 21-acre Founder's Trail Sanctuary are owned by the society, while the 67-acre Collins Sanctuary is owned by the Oregon Parks Foundation but managed and maintained by the society for public use and enjoyment. Founded in 1902, the Audubon Society of Portland maintains its offices and Wildlife Care Center at the sanctuary as well as a visitor center, nature library, bookstore, and gift shop. There are hiking trails throughout the sanctuary, and the society offers guided tours and a variety of natural history programs and classes for adults and children. The society has about 7,000 members.

The fun: Hike the short trail to the pond. It begins just behind the visitor center and drops down a bit steeply to Balch Creek, a 3.5-mile stream that

The pebbly skin of the rough-skinned newt is poisonous.

runs through the sanctuary. It will take just a couple of minutes to reach the pond. Signs will help you find the way.

The newts will either be walking along the pond's bottom or floating at or near the surface, where they tend to congregate on warm, sunny days. The pond is a bit murky, so you may have to look closely to spot the newts when they are underwater.

Food and lodging: All services are available in Portland.

Next best: If the newts are being uncooperative, take a walk through the sanctuary forest. You can pick up a free trail map at the nature store. A total of 4 miles of hiking trails traverse old-growth forest and streamside habitat that attracts a variety of migrating songbirds during May.

For more information:

Audubon Society of Portland
5151 NW Cornell Road
Portland, OR 97210
503-292-6855

Come into My Parlor, Said the Flower to the Fly

13

Carnivorous plants lurk in the forest along a busy, scenic coastal highway.

Site: Darlingtonia State Natural Site, 5 miles (10 minutes) north of Florence.

Recommended time: Late May.

Minimum time commitment: 20 minutes, plus driving time.

What to bring: A boardwalk and railing keep visitors from approaching the plants too closely, so a camera with a telephoto lens or close-focusing binoculars will help you get a better look.

Admission fee: None.

Directions: From Florence, drive north on U.S. Highway 101 for 5 miles. Turn right (east) onto Mercer Lake Road at the sign for Darlingtonia Botanical Gardens. The site and parking area are immediately on the right.

The background: Darlingtonia State Natural Site is the only state park set aside as a botanical preserve. The plant protected here is the California pitcher plant. The park gets its name from the plant's scientific moniker *Darlingtonia californica*.

What makes the pitcher plant worthy of its own park is its carnivorous habit. The tubular leaves of *Darlingtonia* end in a hood with a colorful appendage that resembles a flower petal. The nectar produced by the appendage attracts insects and lures them deeper into the bowels of the flower. Unfortunately for the insects, downward-oriented hairs allow them to crawl into the flower but not back out again. They soon find themselves drowning in a pool of liquid located at the bottom of each of the pitcher plant's leaves. Here, they become plant food as bacteria slowly dissolve them, providing the plant with extra nitrogen. This bog-loving plant grows along the coast in northern California and southwestern Oregon.

The fun: From the parking lot, take the short trail through the forest to the boardwalk over the bog. The California pitcher plants grow in abundance right below your feet. An interpretive sign describes these unique plants and their predatory inclinations.

A profusion of carnivorous pitcher plants lurks just off the boardwalk at Darlingtonia State Natural Site, just north of Florence.

Food and lodging: All services are available in Florence.

Next best: If you are too early to see the pitcher plants bloom (May and June), drive up US 101 another 8 miles and explore the tidepools along Devils Elbow beach at Heceta Head Lighthouse State Scenic Viewpoint. Or watch the ocean for migrating gray whales from the headland.

For more information:

Oregon Parks and Recreation Department
1115 Commercial Street NE
Salem, OR 97310
800-551-6949

The summer sun and Yaquina Head Lighthouse attract swarms of visitors to the Oregon coast near Newport. The lighthouse, first lit in 1873, is the state's tallest and second oldest beacon.

Summer

Bright River, Big Bugs

Swarms of enormous salmonflies hatch on the Deschutes River in June, filling the air and the water in an impressive spectacle of newly emergent life.

Site: Mecca Flat, Deschutes River, 14 miles (20 minutes) north of Madras, 75 miles (1.5 hours) south of The Dalles.

Recommended time: Early June.

Minimum time commitment: 2 hours, plus driving time.

What to bring: Hat, sunglasses, sunscreen, hiking boots, magnifying glass.

Admission fee: None.

Directions: From Madras, go north for 12 miles on U.S. Highway 26. Turn right (east) immediately after passing the Shell gas station and just before crossing the Deschutes River. Follow the dirt road that runs along the river for 1.6 miles to the Mecca Flat parking area, just beyond the campground. If you are traveling south on US 26, the turnoff to Mecca Flat is on the left (east) immediately after crossing over the Deschutes River, past the Deschutes Crossing restaurant.

The background: From late May through mid-June, the salmonfly hatch slowly moves up the Deschutes River as the weather—and the water—gets warmer. These large insects provide an impressive mini-spectacle of nature as they emerge from the water, fly through the air, cling to trees and bushes along the riverbanks, and are gobbled up with gusto by the resident trout, which slurp the tasty bugs off the water's surface with a loud splash.

Salmonflies are a large type of stonefly, an aquatic insect that goes through a series of life stages from egg, to nymph, and finally to adult. The salmonflies are in the nymph stage during late spring. They emerge to fly off, mate, and then die—all within a few days. During the hatching process, the nymphs crawl out of the water onto shrubs, trees, and rocks. Their outer shell splits, and the fully formed adult emerges and then flies off in search of a mate. After mating, the females lay their eggs. As the hatch works its way up the river over a period of weeks, these 3-inch-long winged insects seem to be everywhere.

One of the more accessible places in the Deschutes River canyon to see this insect "migration" is at Mecca Flat, adjacent to the Warm Springs Indian

Monster-sized salmonflies hatch in a short-lived frenzy each year on the Deschutes River.

Reservation, where a level riverside trail makes for easy walking.

The fun: Park at Mecca Flat and walk downriver along the trail. Carefully check the brush and trees along the banks for salmonflies that may be clinging to them. Especially watch tree branches that hang over the water. At this time of year, the river's trout population moves in close to the banks to feast on insects that fall into the water. If you hear and see splashes in these areas, it is almost certainly trout eating salmonflies. You will also see the insects flying along the riverbanks and over the water (they are slow, weak fliers), and if you are lucky, perhaps you may even see some emerging from their nymph shell. Salmonflies do not bite or sting, and they are easily picked up for a closer look.

Food and lodging: There is a gas station and market on U.S. Highway 97 at the Mecca Flat turnoff and a restaurant on the north side of the bridge over the Deschutes River. There is a primitive campground at Mecca Flat. It is open to tents and RVs, although it offers no hookups.

Next best: The swarms of salmonflies attract swarms of fly fishers to the Deschutes River. If you are an angler, try fishing the salmonfly hatch for the river's legendary rainbow trout. Some will tell you there is no other fishing quite like it.

For more information:
Oregon Department of Fish and Wildlife
3701 West 13th Street
The Dalles, OR 97058
541-296-4628

It's a Bug's Life

Oregon streams are filled with aquatic insects, a vital link in the food chain between the microscopic creatures they feed on and the fish that feed on them. In a trout stream such as the Deschutes River, there are four important types of aquatic insects: mayflies, stoneflies, caddis flies, and midges. Each goes through a basic life cycle, part of which is lived in the water, the other in the air and on land.

After mating, female insects lay their eggs underwater, on the water's surface, on streamside vegetation, on logs or rocks, or even on the bank, depending on the species. Out of these eggs hatch nymphs, which reside underwater as they grow and evolve into adulthood. During this period, the insects will molt. As they outgrow their skin it splits open, and the insects free themselves from this external skeleton, growing another one within minutes.

After numerous molts, the nymphs crawl out of the water onto rocks or logs and shed their skin for the final time. Then they fly off in what is called the emergence, or hatch. Hatches even of small insects can be magical, with clouds of fluttering bugs suddenly appearing over the stream's surface, struggling to fly. Those that fail in their first attempt and land in the water are often gulped down by lurking trout.

Caddis flies and midges go through an additional life stage called the pupal stage. They develop a covering, attach themselves to a rock, stick, or other underwater object, and then emerge several weeks later, much as a butterfly breaks out of its chrysalis.

Once airborne, the insect's job is to reproduce. Mayflies mate in the air. Stoneflies and caddis flies mate on the ground. Midges mate anywhere. With that task complete, the females return to the water to lay their eggs. And with that, the cycle comes full circle. ∎

Seabird Condo 15

The largest nesting colony of common murres south of Alaska and the largest tufted puffin colony in Oregon are found on a small group of rocks just off the north coast.

Site: Three Arch Rocks National Wildlife Refuge, 8.5 miles (15 minutes) west of Tillamook.

Recommended time: Mid-June.

Minimum time commitment: 1 hour, plus driving time.

What to bring: A spotting scope is a necessity here because of the distance to the refuge. The coast of Oregon can be cold, rainy, and windy any time of the year, so bring a warm jacket, hat, and rain gear just in case, along with a bird identification guide.

Admission fee: None.

Directions: From U.S. Highway 101 in Tillamook, go west and then south for 8.5 miles on the Netarts Highway, following signs to Oceanside and Three

Common murres are the most numerous nesting shorebirds on the Oregon Coast. Some 200,000 nest at Three Arch Rocks National Wildlife Refuge.

Tufted puffins nest in burrows in which they lay a single egg. Anywhere from 3,000 to 4,000 nest at Three Arch Rocks.

Capes Scenic Drive. At Oceanside, turn left into the Oceanside Beach State Recreation Site parking lot.

The background: Three Arch Rocks National Wildlife Refuge is one of the six national wildlife refuges managed by the U.S. Fish and Wildlife Service that make up the Oregon Coastal Refuges Complex. Comprised of three large rocks and six smaller ones, the 17-acre refuge rises 300 feet above the ocean's surface just half a mile off the coast at Oceanside. It was established in 1907 by President Theodore Roosevelt and was the first national wildlife refuge created west of the Mississippi River.

This refuge provides nesting habitat for over 200,000 common murres, the largest nesting colony of this sea bird south of Alaska. It is also home to the largest colony of tufted puffins in Oregon, with anywhere from 2,000 to 4,000 birds. Other sea birds that nest on the cliffs and crevices of this rocky refuge include pigeon guillemots, storm petrels, and Brandt's and pelagic cormorants. It is used as a pupping and resting area by Steller sea lions, California sea lions, and harbor seals.

The public is not allowed to enter the refuge, which is part of the Oregon Islands Wilderness, but the birds can be viewed from the mainland.

The fun: The best viewing is from Oceanside Beach State Recreation Site in Oceanside. Set up your spotting scope at the edge of the parking lot or on the

Sharing the Space

When over 200,000 birds share nesting space on a rock in the ocean, a little cooperation is in order. In the case of the various species of birds that nest on offshore rocks, such as those at Three Arch Rocks National Wildlife Refuge, the problem is solved by divvying up the microhabitats found there.

The common murre, the most populous of nesting sea birds on the Oregon coast, prefers living on exposed cliffs, where each female lays a single egg. The tufted puffin digs a 3- to 6-foot-deep underground tunnel, where it also lays one egg. Because the rhinoceros auklet is mostly nocturnal, it is not often seen at nesting colonies. It digs a burrow in a grassy slope. The black oystercatcher likes the bases of cliffs, where it hollows out a nesting spot and lines it with pebbles.

Two species of cormorants—Brandt's and double-crested—nest on slopes or flat rocks. The Brandt's cormorant builds its nest of sticks, while the double-crested cormorant adds feathers and bones to the mix. The pelagic cormorant prefers steep cliffs and glues its nest of grass and seaweed together with its droppings.

The pigeon guillemot hides its nest in rock crevices or in burrows, while western and glaucous-winged gulls prefer to settle on flat rocks and shallow slopes. The storm petrel lays a single egg in a burrow or rock crevice.

Offshore rocks are busy places in the spring and summer, swarming with many thousands of nesting birds. With nesting sites so dear amidst the vast ocean, these various species of sea birds have evolved breeding behaviors to allow the many to nest on the few. ■

beach and scan the cliffs for sea birds. You will be able to see birds taking off and landing on the rocks as well as birds swimming and diving at their base. Also, carefully watch the smaller, adjacent rocks and the water surrounding them for seals and sea lions. If you have access to a boat, it is permissible to watch the refuge's wildlife from the water as long as you do not approach the rocks closer than 500 feet.

Food and lodging: Food, lodging, and groceries are available in Oceanside. All services are available in Tillamook.

Next best: Another Oregon coastal wildlife refuge, Cape Meares National Wildlife Refuge, is just up the road from Oceanside. From Oceanside Beach State Recreation Site, drive 0.2 mile south and turn left (north) onto Cape Meares Loop Road. Go 2.4 miles and turn left (west) at the sign for Cape

Meares State Scenic Viewpoint and Cape Meares National Wildlife Refuge. Continue 0.5 mile to the parking lot. There is an interpretive kiosk and hiking trails. This refuge has coastal old-growth forest and cliffs used by nesting seabirds. There is an excellent view of Three Arch Rocks National Wildlife Refuge from the parking lot, although it is too far away to see its wildlife.

For more information:

Oregon Coastal Refuges Complex
U.S. Fish and Wildlife Service
2127 SE OSU Drive
Newport, OR 97365
541-867-4550

Water Bird Way Station 16

Each summer, large concentrations of water birds come to nest at this oasis in the desert, where they are easily observed.

Site: Summer Lake Wildlife Area, 109 miles (2.5 hours) southeast of Bend.
Recommended time: Mid-June.
Minimum time commitment: 2 hours, plus driving time.
What to bring: Binoculars or spotting scope, bird identification guide, camera with telephoto lens.
Admission fee: None.
Directions: From Bend, drive south 33 miles on U.S. Highway 97 to the junction with Oregon Highway 31. Go southeast on OR 31 for 75 miles to the town of Summer Lake. The wildlife area entrance is 1.3 miles south of town on the east side of OR 31.
The background: This 18,677-acre wetland is managed by the Oregon Department of Fish and Wildlife as a refuge for breeding and migratory waterfowl and shorebirds. A series of dikes and canals draws water from the Ana River, which flows through the wildlife area. Water from these canals is used to provide wetlands for birds and other wildlife in a desert region that would otherwise offer very little of this important type of habitat.

As many as 250 species of birds can be seen at the wildlife area, including American avocets, sandhill cranes, Canada geese, great blue herons, long-billed

Summer Lake Wildlife Area

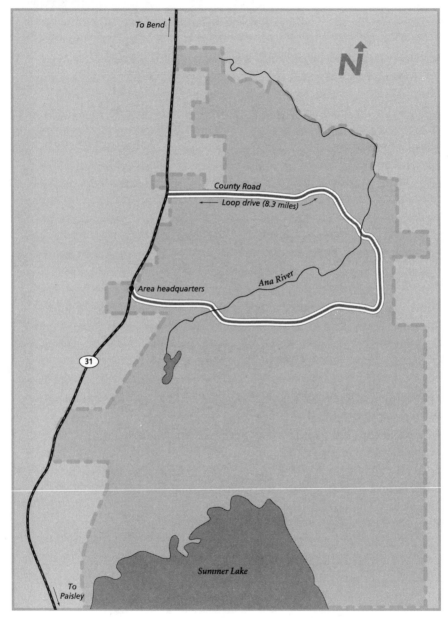

curlews, tundra swans, American white pelicans, and snowy egrets.

An 8.3-mile driving tour leads through the heart of the refuge marshlands, allowing visitors a relatively close approach to waterfowl. Because of this, the Summer Lake Wildlife Area often provides better viewing of nesting waterfowl than other larger, less accessible refuges.

The wildlife area gets its name from the large, shallow, alkaline lake that lies just outside its southern boundary.

The fun: The earlier you arrive in the morning the better. Start the road tour at the refuge headquarters, where you can pick up a map to the area. Follow the signs as you drive slowly through tall marsh grass and reeds and between ponds, looking carefully for ducks and coots with their young swimming dutifully behind. Just past the first campground is a parking area. It is a good place to stop and scan the surrounding ponds for Canada geese, mallards, pintails, gadwalls, shovelers, and other waterfowl. Pods of large white birds in the distance are probably American white pelicans.

As you continue on, the road begins to parallel Link Canal. Pelicans often ply these canals, affording reasonably good opportunities to get an up-close look before they fly off. Great blue herons are also readily seen here. Coot nests, built on hummocks in the open water, are sometimes visible as well.

The final leg of the road tour runs along Schoolhouse Lake. Carefully scan the rocky flats on the west side of the road for American avocets sitting

Careful observers at Summer Lake Wildlife Area may spot nesting American avocets.

serenely on the ground. They are probably sitting on nests. If you stop and quietly watch them for a while (but do not get out of the car), you are likely to see newborn chicks teetering around on wobbly legs. From Schoolhouse Lake, follow the road through a drier environment to the junction with a county road. Go left (west) here and return to the town of Summer Lake.

Food and lodging: There is a general store, gas station, and small motel in Summer Lake. A cottonwood-lined rest area on the east side of the highway just as you enter town makes a nice spot for lunch. There are four no-frills campgrounds at the wildlife area.

Next best: For a bird's-eye view of Summer Lake and the surrounding desert, drive up Forest Road 2901 (on the west side of OR 31 about 4 miles north of Summer Lake) for about 15 miles, turn off onto FR 034, and go 2 miles to Fremont Point.

For more information:
Summer Lake Wildlife Area
36981 Highway 31
Summer Lake, OR 97640
541-943-3152

Elk in Repose

Early summer finds cow Roosevelt elk and their calves grazing in a wet meadow just a few miles from the shores of the Pacific Ocean.

Site: Dean Creek Elk Viewing Area, 3.2 miles (5 minutes) east of Reedsport.
Recommended time: Late June.
Minimum time commitment: 45 minutes, plus driving time.
What to bring: Binoculars or spotting scope. (Or use the free spotting scope mounted on the viewing deck at the interpretive facility.)
Admission fee: None.
Directions: From Reedsport, go 3.2 miles east on Oregon Highway 38 to the interpretive facility on the right (south) side of the road. From Interstate 5, 12 miles south of Cottage Grove, take exit 162 and head west on Oregon Highway 99, then OR 38, for 53 miles to the elk viewing area.
The background: In the 1930s, construction of OR 38 blocked the flooding of the Dean Creek meadows that usually resulted from the influence of Pacific tides on the Umpqua River. At the same time, local ranchers and farm-

Interpretive panels at Dean Creek Elk Viewing Area explain its history, both human and natural.

ers diked the meadows in order to grow crops. Local elk populations discovered these ready-made fields of food and, instead of moving into the forest and upland meadows to feed, began foraging around Dean Creek.

Today a resident herd of 60 to 100 Roosevelt elk wanders this 1,040-acre tract of woodland, wetland, and pasture. The area is now managed by the Bureau of Land Management for the benefit of waterfowl and other wildlife. The BLM mows and fertilizes pastures to improve and increase the amount and quality of forage available for the elk.

The fun: Start at the interpretive facility. A series of panels tells about elk and the environment of the Dean Creek area. Use the spotting scope at the facility or your own binoculars or spotting scope to scan the area. You may spot elk anywhere throughout the meadows. They may be lying down, so do not neglect to carefully peruse the tall grass. The viewing area stretches almost 3 miles along the south side of the road, so be sure and drive its length. There are turnouts along the way where you can stop to watch. Morning and evening are the best viewing times, but elk may be out at any time of day.

Food and lodging: All services are available in Reedsport.

Next best: Visit from mid-September to early October to hear (and maybe see) bugling bull elk during the rut.

For more information:

Bureau of Land Management
Coos Bay District
1300 Airport Lane
North Bend, OR 97459
541-756-0100

Snakes Alive

18

For something a bit different, try an afternoon of snake watching at a wildlife area just outside the university town of Eugene. On a warm sunny afternoon, you can spot dozens of harmless garter snakes along a soggy fence row.

Site: Fisher Butte Unit, Fern Ridge Wildlife Area, 3 miles (15 minutes) west of Eugene.

Recommended time: Early July.

Minimum time commitment: 1 hour, plus driving time.

What to bring: Rubber boots.

Admission fee: None.

Directions: From the city limits of Eugene, drive 3 miles west on Oregon Highway 126. Park at the signed parking area on the right (north) side of the highway.

The background: Managed by the Oregon Department of Fish and Wildlife, the 5,103-acre Fern Ridge Wildlife Area is nestled against the east, south, and west shores of Fern Ridge Reservoir. The area consists primarily of wetlands.

In addition to the 250 species of birds that are found here throughout the course of the year, dozens of garter snakes gather in this relatively concentrated area. Three species of garter snakes live in western Oregon: common, western terrestrial, and western aquatic. These harmless reptiles can be identified by a yellowish stripe down their backs and are frequently found around water.

The fun: From the parking area, walk north up the gravel road for about 0.2 mile to the gate. Turn left and walk along the fencerow, watching the ground along both sides of the path. The fence row will be on your right, and an open, marshy area will be on your left.

The snakes often sun themselves on the path but slither quickly out of sight as they hear you approach. You may also hear them moving through the grass as you pass by. After fleeing a short distance, the snakes will typically stop, allowing a close approach if you move slowly and quietly.

It is possible to see several dozen garter snakes here in a short period of time.

Food and lodging: All services are available in Eugene.

Next best: If birds appeal to you more than snakes, try visiting here in late

The wet meadow and tall grasses of the Fisher Butte Unit of Fern Ridge Wildlife Area comprise perfect habitat for colorful garter snakes.

October or November, when large concentrations of shorebirds and waterfowl congregate in open water and marshlands.

For more information:
Fern Ridge Wildlife Area
26969 Cantrell Road
Eugene, OR 97402
541-935-2591

Butterfly Byway  19

The warm summer sun brings out the butterflies along this scenic drive through a national forest in central Oregon.

Site: Big Summit Prairie, Ochoco National Forest, 35 miles (45 minutes) east of Prineville.
Recommended time: Mid-July.
Minimum time commitment: 2 to 4 hours.
What to bring: Binoculars, camera with telephoto lens, butterfly field guide, picnic lunch and blanket.

Big Summit Prairie, Ochoco National Forest

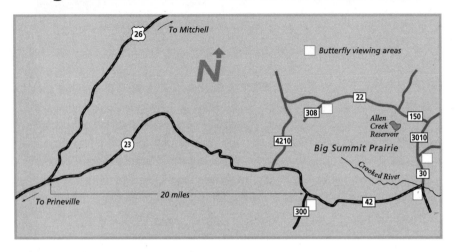

Admission fee: None.

Directions: From Prineville, drive east on U.S. Highway 26 for 15 miles. Bear right at the fork marked with a sign for the Ochoco Ranger Station and Ochoco Creek onto County Road 23. It eventually becomes Forest Road 42. Continue into the Ochoco National Forest on FR 42 for 20 miles. Turn right onto FR 300. Park here along the open meadow of Big Summit Prairie.

The background: Butterflies go with flowers the way bees go with honey. Anywhere there are flowers, there are likely to be butterflies. But some places are known to be better butterfly-watching spots than others. One of those is Big Summit Prairie in the 848,000-acre Ochoco National Forest.

Big Summit Prairie is a high-country meadow surrounded by a forest of ponderosa pines. Spring and summer bring the blossoming of such wildflowers as bitterroot, Oregon checkermallow, paintbrush, Peck's mariposa lily, shooting star, camas, and Missouri iris. With the arrival of the flowers come the butterflies.

The fun: Park at the junction of FR 42 and FR 300 by Dudley Creek, where you will be nearly surrounded by flower-strewn meadows. Butterfly watching is best between 9 A.M. and 4 P.M., when they are most likely to be flying around feeding on the nectar of the flowers. And you will be better off if you let them come to you rather than chasing after them. So find a comfortable spot, lay out your blanket, sit quietly, and watch the surrounding meadow. Any disturbance your arrival may have caused the meadow's inhabitants will soon pass, and you will begin to see these delicate creatures fluttering daintily from flower to flower, particularly the common but striking Oregon swallowtail.

To maximize your butterfly watching, continue east on FR 42 from its junction with FR 300. Drive 7 miles to the junction with FR 30. The Crooked River crosses the road here, and wetland-loving wildflowers offer more butterfly-watching opportunities. From here, go left (north) on FR 30 for 1.5 miles to the Cold Springs meadow area, where larkspur, lilies, and other flowers attract butterflies. Then continue north on FR 30 for 0.5 mile, bear left onto FR 3010, go 2 miles, and turn left onto FR 150. Follow FR 150 west for about 3 miles and bear left onto FR 22. Go 5 miles to Indian Creek. There, FR 308 angles off to the left into a series of wildflower meadows similar to those at Dudley Creek. To finish the trip, continue west on FR 22 for 1 mile, turn left onto FR 4210, and then drive 4 miles to rejoin FR 42. Turn right (west) to get back to US 26.

You can pick up a map of the forest and a very helpful brochure entitled "Wildflowers of Big Summit Prairie" at the Ochoco National Forest headquarters on the south side of US 26 at the east end of Prineville. Much of Big Summit Prairie is privately owned. However, the boundaries between public and private lands are fairly well marked.

Food and lodging: All services are available in Prineville.

Next best: Butterfly watching and wildflower identification go hand in hand, so bring your flower field guide, too. The wildflowers bloom on Big Summit Prairie from April through July.

For more information:
Ochoco National Forest
USDA Forest Service
3160 NE Third Street
Prineville, OR 97754
541-416-6500

Wildflower expanses on Big Summit Prairie attract an array of butterfly species, including the Oregon swallowtail.

Alpine Bouquet

An extravaganza of high-country wildflowers greets hikers on this easy, accessible trail in the Cascade Mountains.

Site: Iron Mountain Trail, 34 miles (40 minutes) east of Sweet Home.

Recommended time: Mid-July.

Minimum time commitment: 4 hours, plus driving time.

What to bring: Binoculars, flower and tree identification guidebooks, magnifying glass, camera with close-up lens, sturdy hiking boots, day pack, lunch, water (there is no water available on the mountain). Although the weather at this time of year is typically warm, sunny, and conducive to T-shirts and shorts, it can sometimes be windy at the summit. It is wise to bring a windbreaker or light sweater along, just in case.

Admission fee: A Trail Park Pass is required at this trailhead. You can purchase a day pass for $3 or a season pass for $25 from Forest Service offices and many sporting goods stores.

Directions: From the city of Sweet Home, drive 34 miles east on U.S. Highway 20 to the Tombstone Pass area. Turn right (south) onto Forest Road 15 and drive 0.25 mile to the trailhead. To reach the upper parking area, take Civil Road (FR 035) on the north side of the highway about 1.5 miles west of Tombstone Pass. Follow it 2.9 miles to the parking area.

The background: One of Oregon's best and most accessible displays of high-meadow wildflowers is found on 5,455-foot Iron Mountain, in the heart of the Cascade Range. Iron Mountain Trail takes visitors through a cool forest of Douglas-fir and western hemlock before leading into the upper flower-strewn meadows.

Iron Mountain area is known for its botanical diversity. Over 300 species of wildflowers—almost every species that grows in the western Cascade Mountains—may be seen along the Iron Mountain Trail. Among them are crimson columbine, red gilia, scarlet delphinium, paintbrush, and bear grass. Along with nearby Cone Peak, South Peak, and Echo Mountain, Iron Mountain features among the greatest variety of coniferous tree species in Oregon, including noble fir, grand fir, white fir, subalpine fir, western yew, Pacific silver fir, western white pine, western hemlock, mountain hemlock, Engelmann spruce, and Alaska cedar.

As an added bonus, Iron Mountain's gaudy spectacle of wildflowers

Iron Mountain, in the Cascade Range, boasts one of Oregon's most spectacular and accessible displays of alpine wildflowers. Among the species growing there are the crimson columbine (top) and Tolmie's pussy ears.

attracts large numbers of hummingbirds and colorful butterflies. Views from the fire lookout at the summit take in a broad expanse of the Cascade Mountains.

The fun: To fully enjoy the forest and the meadow wildflowers, park at the trailhead on FR 15 and hike the 1.6-mile Iron Mountain Trail to the summit through a variety of habitat types, each with its own distinctive species of flowers. The trail is moderately steep.

Food and lodging: Mountain House, 10 miles west of Iron Mountain on US 20, serves meals. A small selection of groceries is also available, but no lodging or gas.

Next best: To make the trip shorter and less strenuous, drive to the upper parking area and walk the final half mile through the meadows to the summit. You will miss the forested section, but the best show of wildflowers is on the upper mountain.

For more information:
Willamette National Forest
Sweet Home Ranger District
3225 Highway 20
Sweet Home, OR 97386
541-367-5168

Seals on the Rocks  21

As many as 100 harbor seals at a time haul out to rest and bask in the sun on offshore rocks during the summer months.

Site: Strawberry Hill at Neptune State Scenic Viewpoint, 27 miles (30 minutes) south of Newport.

Recommended time: Late July.

Minimum time commitment: 30 minutes, plus driving time.

What to bring: Spotting scope or binoculars.

Admission fee: None.

Directions: From Newport, drive south on U.S. Highway 101 for 26.8 miles (3.8 miles south of Yachats). The parking area for Strawberry Hill is on the right (west).

The background: A common denizen of the Oregon Coast, harbor seals feed while the tide is high and then haul out onto the rocks just offshore from

During the summer, as many as 100 harbor seals haul out on the rocks at Neptune State Scenic Viewpoint to bask in the sun at low tide.

Strawberry Hill to bask in the sun and rest during low tide. You may see as many as 100 seals at any given time during the summer.

Harbor seals eat mostly fish and sometimes learn to raid the nets of commercial fishermen, making the animals unpopular with people who make a living from the sea. They can dive as deep as 300 feet and remain underwater for almost half an hour. As marine mammals, they are protected by federal law. You should avoid disturbing them and remain at least 100 feet away from them at all times.

The fun: From the viewpoint, you can easily scan the rocks below with binoculars or spotting scope for seals. You will find them lying on the rocks as well as swimming in the surrounding water, where often only their heads poke above the surface.

Food and lodging: Lodging, food, gas, and groceries are available in Yachats, 3.8 miles north on US 101.

Next best: You can spot seals resting off Strawberry Hill at any time of the year, although more congregate during the summer. There are also excellent tidepools here. Be careful not to disturb basking seals during your explorations.

For more information:

Oregon Parks and Recreation Department
1115 Commercial Street NE
Salem, OR 97310
800-551-6949

Marine
Garden Bounty

22

Explore the wonders of tidepool life at the "marine gardens" of Yaquina Head.

Site: Yaquina Head Outstanding Natural Area, 3.5 miles (10 minutes) north of Newport.

Recommended time: Late July.

Minimum time commitment: 3 hours, plus driving time.

What to bring: Binoculars, bird identification guide, field guide to tidal life (*Guide to Oregon's Intertidal Habitats* is available for $5 from the Oregon Department of Fish and Wildlife, 503-872-5264), camera, close-up and telephoto lenses with polarizing filter to cut glare from the water when photographing tidepool creatures, footwear with nonslip soles for walking on slippery rocks, windbreaker.

Admission fee: $5 per vehicle daily.

Directions: From Newport, drive 3 miles north on U.S. Highway 101. Turn left (west) onto Lighthouse Drive at the sign for the Yaquina Head Outstanding Natural Area. Drive 0.4 mile to the Yaquina Head Interpretive Center (you pass through a pay station first). To reach the lighthouse and trail to Cobble Beach and the tidepools, continue past the interpretive center for 0.3 mile to the parking area. To reach the manmade Quarry Cove Tide Pools, follow Lighthouse Drive 0.3 mile from the US 101 turnoff and turn left at the sign. Go 0.2 mile to the parking lot and trailhead.

The background: In 1980, Congress designated 100 acres of this spectacular headland as an Outstanding Natural Area to protect its scenic, recreational, educational, and ecological values. Expansive views of the ocean and coastline, as well as the scenic Yaquina Head Lighthouse, have attracted visitors here for years. The lighthouse, first lit in 1873, is Oregon's second oldest and, at 93 feet, its tallest. But Yaquina Head is best known for its tidepools, often referred to as "marine gardens."

At low tide, rock outcroppings along Cobble Beach on the south side of the headland become a series of pools filled with barnacles, anemones, sea stars, small fish, sea urchins, crabs, and a host of other sea creatures. In the spring and summer, shorebirds nest on the headland's steep cliffs, while harbor seals ply the area's waters.

Yaquina Head Outstanding Natural Area

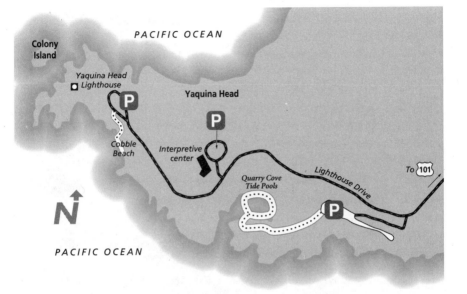

Between 1992 and 1994, the Bureau of Land Management, which manages the area, constructed an artificial intertidal area in a former rock quarry. It is accessible via a paved trail, allowing wheelchair users and others with limited mobility the opportunity to explore the wonders of a marine garden. The Yaquina Head Interpretive Center features exhibits on the intertidal ocean environment and the history of the Yaquina Head Lighthouse, which is open to the public for daily tours. The visitor center is open from 10 A.M. to 6 P.M. May 15 through October 31 and 10 A.M. to 4 P.M. from November 1 through May 14. Yaquina Head Outstanding Natural Area is open daily from dawn to dusk.

The fun: First, consult a tide table, available at sporting goods stores, hardware stores, and many other shops on the coast, to determine when low tides occur. To get the most time to explore the tidepools, start one hour before low tide.

For some serious exploration, drive to the parking lot at the Yaquina Head Lighthouse and take the steep but short set of stairs on the south side of the lot down to Cobble Beach and its tidepools. Scramble among the rocks and look closely and carefully into each pool. Take your time, because many intertidal animals are well camouflaged. If you sit quietly and peer into a tidepool for at least a minute, you will begin to see the variety of animals that live there as they move about on their daily business. Do not forget to watch the cliffs

The shoreline at Yaquina Head Outstanding Natural Area offers excellent examples of marine gardens for the inquisitive to explore.

for sea birds and the rocks of the offshore islands for seals.

If you have less time available or want a less strenuous outing, go to the Quarry Cove Intertidal Area and walk the paved trail through these artificial marine gardens. Although they are manmade, they are connected to the sea and contain the same animals that the natural tidepools have.

Stay alert while exploring tidepools. Large, unexpected waves (called "sneaker" waves) can come seemingly from out of nowhere. They are especially dangerous when they pick up and toss pieces of driftwood. There is an old saying on the Oregon coast that goes "never turn your back on the ocean."

Food and lodging: All services are available in Newport.

Next best: Other popular tidepooling areas include Ecola State Park, Cape Perpetua, Otter Rock, Haystack Rock, and Yachats, Devil's Punch Bowl and Seal Rock state recreation areas.

For more information:

Yaquina Head Outstanding Natural Area
Bureau of Land Management
P.O. Box 936
Newport, OR 97365
541-574-3100

A Tidepool Primer

Standing on the rocky Oregon shoreline, you might think that it is simply a place where sea meets land. But in fact, there is a complex hierarchy of habitat based on how often and to what depth each segment of shoreline is covered by water. That, in turn, is governed by the daily cycles of low and high tides.

Tides are the result of the gravitational pull of the moon and sun on the earth and its oceans. There are two low tides and two high tides every 24 hours and 50 minutes. This regular rise and fall of the ocean covers different parts of the shoreline with different depths of water for different amounts of time each day, resulting in a variety of habitats whose inhabitants have evolved to survive within those varying degrees of "wetness."

There are four basic life zones along the shoreline: low-tide zone, middle-tide zone, high-tide zone, and spray zone. The low-tide zone is an area that is exposed for only a short period of time each day, at low-tide. As you would expect, it has the greatest abundance and variety of sea life, including red sea cucumbers, purple sea urchins, sea palms, feather boas, sunflower sea stars, and giant Pacific chitons. Lots of red-colored seaweed is a sure sign that you are in the low-tide zone.

The middle-tide zone is exposed by the outgoing tide at least once a day— a bit more than the low-tide zone—and it also harbors lots of sea life, including green anemones, common sea stars, hermit crabs, and mussels. If most of the seaweed is green, you are probably in the middle-tide zone.

Farther inland, the high-tide zone is only underwater during periods of high tide, and therefore it is exposed to the air for long periods of time. Fewer sea animals and plants are able to exist in this zone. Some that can are black turban snails, rockweed, purple shore crabs, and clumps of small anemones. Yellow seaweed is a good indicator that you are in the high-tide zone.

Finally, the most difficult place for sea life to survive is in the spray zone, where the only seawater comes from the splashing of waves. Limpets and barnacles are an example of the handful of marine creatures that are able to make a life here.

These varied environments along Oregon's shoreline make exploring the tidepools and their inhabitants all the more interesting—and make it all the more important that you take care not to damage this fragile environment. Do not take sea stars or any other animals home with you; walk carefully so as not to step on any living creatures; and if you do pick anything up for a closer look, put it back in the same place you found it. A tidepool animal put into a zone it is not adapted to will not last long! ∎

Up and Over

Watch migrating steelhead, which are a type of salmon and one of the Pacific Northwest's premier game fish, through viewing windows as they ascend the fish ladder over Bonneville Dam during their annual spawning run up the Columbia River.

Site: Bradford Island Visitor Center, Bonneville Dam, 36 miles (40 minutes) east of Portland.

Recommended time: Early August.

Minimum time commitment: 2 hours, plus driving time.

What to bring: Camera with fast film for taking pictures of fish swimming by the viewing windows, fish identification guide. A free fish identification booklet is available at the visitor center information desk.

Admission fee: None.

Directions: From Portland, drive 36 miles east on Interstate 84. Take exit 40. At the stop sign, turn left and follow the signs a little over 1 mile through the fish hatchery and around the dam's first powerhouse to the visitor center.

The background: Built on the Columbia River between 1933 and 1937 by the U.S. Army Corps of Engineers at a cost of $88.4 million, Bonneville Dam produces over 1 million kilowatts of power—enough to supply all the electricity needs of about 500,000 homes for a year.

Because the dam represents a barrier to salmon, steelhead, and other species of fish that migrate upstream to spawn each year, fish ladders have been installed to provide a way for fish to climb over the dam. These fish ladders are made up of cross barriers called weirs that form a series of ascending pools. Openings at the bottom of the weirs allow the fish to swim over the dam, one pool at a time, and into the reservoir above. Over the course of a year, between 700,000 and 1 million migrating salmon and steelhead pass upstream over the dam.

Bonneville Dam is one of eight dams built and owned by the federal government on the Columbia and Snake Rivers.

The fun: The five-story Bradford Island Visitor Center, located on Bradford Island in the middle of the Columbia River, features interpretive exhibits, a theater, fish-viewing windows, and an observation deck with a bird's-eye view of the Bradford Island Fish Ladder.

Begin on the main level where the interpretive exhibits are located, includ-

Bonneville Dam

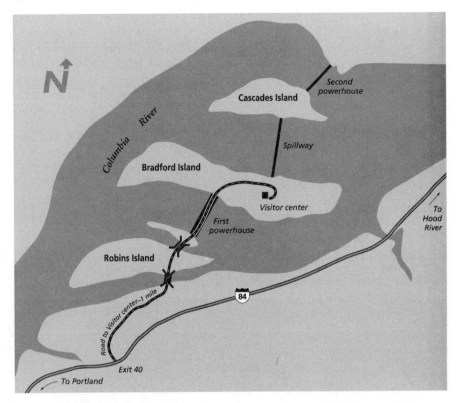

ing displays on the history of the region and on how hydropower facilities work. There is also a small bookstore on this level.

Outside, on Level 3, you can look down on the Bradford Island Fish Ladder to get an idea of how it functions and is constructed.

But to see steelhead, you will want to head to Level 1, where a series of viewing windows stretch across the far wall and give you an underwater view of the fish ladder's pools. When the fish are moving, it will not take long to see quite a few. Steelhead passing over the dam average about 10 pounds, although you may see 20-pounders as well. Steelhead can reach a weight of 42 pounds, but fish that large are rarely seen at the dam. You will also find exhibits about the various other species of fish that migrate over the dam on this level, including chinook, coho, and sockeye salmon; American shad; and Pacific lamprey. Although August is the peak time for migrating steelhead, you are also likely to see some of these other species at this time as well.

The visitor center is open from 9 A.M. to 5 P.M. every day except Christmas, Thanksgiving, and New Year's Day.

Six different species of anadromous fish migrate over Bonneville Dam via the fish ladder during the course of the year.

Food and lodging: All services are available in the community of Cascade Locks, 4 miles east of Bonneville Dam on I-84, off exit 44.

Next best: Peak migration time for seeing chinook and coho salmon is September; for sockeye salmon and American shad, it is June. Pacific lamprey pass through from June through August.

For more information:
Bonneville Lock and Dam
U.S. Army Corps of Engineers
Cascade Locks, OR 97014
541-374-8820

Where the Deer and the Antelope Play   24

Large concentrations of pronghorn antelope congregate here during summer and early fall. There are good chances of spotting bighorn sheep as well.

Site: Hart Mountain National Antelope Refuge, 78 miles (2 hours) northeast of Lakeview.

Recommended time: Mid-August.

Minimum time commitment: Because of its remoteness and the many sights to see, it is best to devote at least an entire weekend. If driving time is significant, you may want to allow a total of 3 days.

What to bring: Camping gear, food and water, binoculars or spotting scope, camera with telephoto lens, sturdy hiking boots, field guides, hat for protection from the sun.

Admission fee: None.

Directions: From Lakeview, drive 5 miles north on U.S. Highway 395. Turn right (east) onto Oregon Highway 140 and go 29 miles. Turn left (north) onto County Road 310 and drive 19 miles to Plush. From there, follow CR 312 for 25 miles to the refuge headquarters. The road into the refuge is steep, narrow, and winding in places, so drive carefully.

The background: Established in 1936 to provide spring, summer, and fall habitat for pronghorn antelope, this 275,000-acre refuge is located in Oregon's Great Basin Desert and is managed by the U.S. Fish and Wildlife Service. The rugged rimrock on its west side rises 3,600 feet from the desert floor, while

Hart Mountain National Antelope Refuge

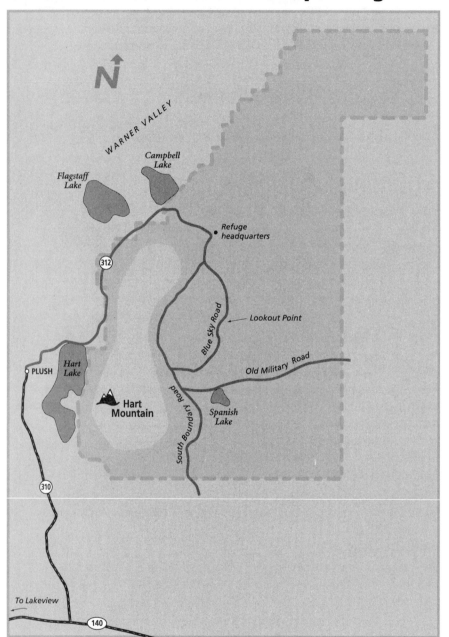

ridges and hills on the east side keep a low and gentle profile. In between, you will find rangelands, aspen groves, streams, numerous springs, intermittent lakes, and precipitous desert mountain terrain.

Because of its high-quality habitat and relatively abundant water supply, the refuge is a haven for a variety of desert wildlife. Its wide-open spaces make wildlife easy to spot over great distances.

Although the refuge is most famous for its antelope, its more remote and rugged areas are home to bighorn sheep; mule deer are also common. Small animals often spotted by visitors include coyotes, blacktail jackrabbits, and Belding's ground squirrels. About 200 species of birds are known to inhabit the area, including burrowing owls, sage grouse, golden eagles, and prairie falcons.

The fun: Begin at the headquarters, where you can stop at the visitors room (open 24 hours a day) to pick up information and look at a small display of wildlife exhibits.

The best bet for spotting antelope is to visit the open country on the refuge's southern half. A prime location to begin your search is Lookout Point. To get there, drive 9 miles south from the refuge headquarters, past the turnoff to Frenchglen, and bear left at the fork onto Blue Sky Road. The right-hand fork takes you to Hot Springs Campground. Park in the lot and scan the surrounding rangeland with binoculars or a spotting scope. Because the animals may be off in the distance, the best way to spot them is by looking for their characteristic white rump patch, which tends to stand out from the grays and greens of the open range.

Large herds of pronghorn antelope gather at Hart Mountain National Antelope Refuge during the summer.

From there, continue south on Blue Sky Road, watching toward the east as you go. Antelope spotting is best done from a vehicle, because they are wide-ranging animals capable of speeds up to 70 miles per hour. You need to be able to cover as much ground as they do.

You will find the largest herds in the Spanish Flat area east of the South Boundary Road. From Lookout Point, drive south on Blue Sky Road for 7 miles and turn left (south) onto South Boundary Road. Go 1.5 miles to the Old Military Road and turn left (east). Spanish Lake is 2 miles to the east. Roads in the Spanish Flat area are best traveled with a high-clearance vehicle.

Food and lodging: All services are available in Lakeview. In Plush, you will find gas and a small convenience store. Undeveloped campsites are available on the refuge at Hot Springs Campground. A dip in the enclosed hot springs here is a great way to unwind after a day of exploring.

Next best: The Warner Wetlands, located along the western edge of the refuge, is an excellent area for watching birds, especially waterfowl.

For more information:
Sheldon–Hart Mountain Refuges
U.S. Fish and Wildlife Service
P.O. Box 111
Lakeview, OR 97630
541-947-3315

Journey to the Stars  25

View planets, galaxies, nebula, and other heavenly bodies at this modern observatory in the desert.

Site: Pine Mountain Observatory, 35 miles (40 minutes) east of Bend.
Recommended time: Mid-August.
Minimum time commitment: 4 hours, plus driving time.
What to bring: Warm jacket, hat, flashlight, telescope if you own one, snacks, hot drinks.
Admission fee: Suggested donation of $2 per person.
Directions: From Bend, take U.S. Highway 20 East and drive 26 miles to Millican. Just beyond Millican, turn right (south) onto the gravel road and go 9 miles. At the base of the mountain, take the right fork to the observatory.
The background: Built in 1967 and operated by the University of Oregon as

Visitors can unlock the secrets of the heavens at this modern observatory east of Bend.

an educational and research facility, Pine Mountain Observatory is open to the public on Friday and Saturday evenings from May 28 through September 25.

Astronomical equipment here includes 15-, 24-, and 32-inch telescopes. Observatory staff members conduct public educational programs that include an introduction to the basics of astronomy, a tour of the facility, and the opportunity to look through the 15- and 24-inch telescopes at various objects in the sky.

The fun: Call the observatory first to check on weather conditions. Also, observatory staff members like to have an idea in advance of how many people will be arriving each night.

As you approach the parking lot, dim your headlights because there are likely to be stargazers who have arrived before you. Many amateur astronomers who come here bring their own telescopes. If you do, observatory staff members will put you to work finding interesting sky objects for visitors to look at.

Attend the lecture and slide show covering the basic principles of astronomy and take the opportunity to view stars, planets, galaxies, globular clusters, and other sky objects. Then check out the demonstration of how the 32-inch telescope here creates images of heavenly bodies on a computer screen. Bring a floppy disk with you and you can even bring home a picture of a galaxy to display on your own computer.

The clear desert air makes this location ideal for astronomers, and many visitors make a night of it, searching the skies with telescopes and binoculars until the first rays of dawn peer over the eastern horizon.

Food and lodging: All services are available in Bend. There is an undeveloped campground on Pine Mountain.

Next best: Although dark, moonless skies are the best for sky gazing, do not despair if your schedule only allows a visit on a moonlit weekend. There will still be plenty of objects to look at. And the view of the moon, our closest heavenly body, through these powerful telescopes is spectacular.

For more information:
Pine Mountain Observatory
Bend–Burns Star Route
Bend, OR 97701
541-382-8331

Landscapes Frozen in Time

Oregon's fiery past surrounds visitors at Newberry National Volcanic Monument, smack in the center of a volcano that some suspect is still active.

Site: Newberry National Volcanic Monument, 13 miles (20 minutes) south of Bend.

Recommended time: Late August.

Minimum time commitment: 2 to 6 hours, depending on how many sites you visit.

What to bring: Camera and wide-angle lens for shooting panoramas, rugged hiking boots for walking across lava flows, warm coat for exploring Lava River Cave.

Admission fee: A day pass is $3 per vehicle. A season pass is $25.

Directions: Lava Lands Visitor Center is 13 miles south of Bend on the west side of U.S. Highway 97. Lava River Cave is 1 mile south of the visitor center on the opposite side of the highway. To reach Paulina Peak, the summit of the volcano, drive 12 miles south from the visitor center on US 97. Turn left (east) onto County Road 21 and follow it for 13 miles to the Paulina Visitor Center; then turn right on Forest Road 500 and drive 4 miles to the summit.

The background: Managed by the Forest Service, Newberry National Volcanic Monument was established in 1990 to protect its unique geologic resources. The 56,000-acre area boasts extensive lava flows, lakes, waterfalls, forests, caves, and examples of over 95 percent of the world's volcanic features.

The centerpiece of the monument is Newberry Caldera. Encompassing 500 square miles, it is one of the largest shield-shaped volcanoes in the lower 48 states. Within the center caldera are East and Paulina Lakes. The latter is 250 feet deep, making it one of the deepest lakes in the state. East Lake is about 180 feet deep.

Newberry Caldera erupted as recently as 1,300 years ago and may only be dormant rather than extinct, suggesting the possibility that one day it could shower the surrounding countryside with molten rock and ash, as it once did in the not-so-distant past.

The fun: Start out at the Lava Lands Visitor Center to view the interpretive

Newberry National Volcanic Monument

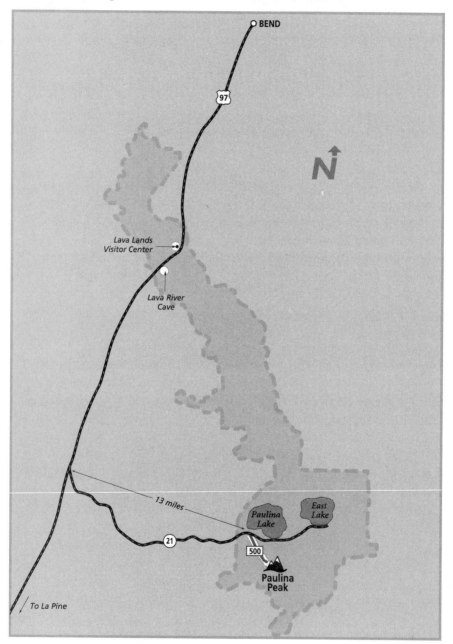

exhibits. Then take the 50-minute shuttle-bus tour to the summit of Lava Butte, a 500-foot cinder cone. The trip costs $2 for adults and teenagers and $1.50 for seniors and children 6 to 12. It includes a talk on geology and a 30-minute break on top to allow time for hiking around the summit crater.

Next, head 1 mile down the highway from the visitor center to Lava River Cave. The cave is a lava tube, created when the outer surface of a lava flow cooled and hardened while the still-molten center oozed out, leaving a hollow tube behind. Lava River Cave has two tunnels, one nearly a mile long and

Born of Fire

The central Oregon landscape and its major features were created largely by fiery volcanic eruptions in the distant, and not-so-distant, past. Pilot Butte—a conical, symmetrical, 4,136-foot-high peak—was formed when cinders and ash were ejected from a volcanic vent. It was a major landmark for pioneers on their way west to settle in the Willamette Valley.

Newberry Crater, now part of Newberry National Volcanic Monument, formed about 500,000 years ago when a series of lava flows emanated from vents on the earth's surface, building up an immense volcano encompassing 500 square miles and rising 4,000 feet above the surrounding desert. In time, the volcano's summit collapsed, creating a caldera that now contains two large, coldwater lakes.

Lava Butte, also part of the national monument, is a cinder cone, formed when a volcanic eruption deposited lava fragments that eventually built up this small conical volcano. Lava Butte rises about 500 feet above the surrounding landscape. Over 6,000 years ago, lava flowing from vents and fissures on the side of Newberry Volcano dammed the nearby Deschutes River, diverting the water from its course at that time and forming a 10-square mile lava field visible today to the west from the summit of Lava Butte.

In some places, lava flows engulfed live trees and the molten rock slowly burned them. As the lava cooled, it left behind "lava casts" of the trees that once grew there.

Another unique aspect of this volcanic landscape is the jet-black obsidian, a type of glass formed when lava with high levels of silica in it cools quickly. Obsidian in central Oregon was collected by the prehistoric inhabitants and used to make knives, arrowheads, and other tools.

Today, the green forest of ponderosa pines and the peaceful mountain scenery belie the geologically violent history of a landscape that at one time was literally on fire. ∎

the other just over 1,500 feet. Inside the tube, you will find large open chambers, piles of rock that have fallen from the ceiling, low ceilings, and sandy stretches. The cave maintains a year-round temperature of 40 degrees Fahrenheit. Entry to the cave costs $3 for adults and $2 for youths 12 to 17. Kids under 12 are admitted free. Lantern rentals are $2. The entire excursion is an easy 2.4-mile (1.5-hour) hike.

Once you return to daylight, dust yourself off and drive south to Paulina Peak, named after a local Indian leader of the 1860s. You can drive to its 7,985-foot summit on a winding road or hike the adjacent trail. Both leave from the Paulina Visitor Center, and both are 4 miles long. At the summit, you will be treated to 360-degree views of the surrounding forest and lava flows from the highest point in the monument. This is the perfect way to punctuate your visit.

Food and lodging: All services are available in Bend, north of the monument, and in La Pine, 2 miles to the south. There are seven campgrounds in the monument as well as two small resorts that offer cabins, general stores, gas, and restaurants.

Next best: From the Lava Lands Visitor Center, drive 9.5 miles north on US 97 to the High Desert Museum to learn about the natural and human history of the western intermountain desert (see Trip 1).

For more information:

Lava Lands Visitor Center
58201 South Highway 97
Bend, OR 97707
541-593-2421

Autumn

Ice Is Nice
and Will Suffice

27

Sweeping views of a glacier, complete with crevasses and ice cliffs, may be had from a ridgetop overlook just a short hike from your vehicle.

Site: Cooper Spur, Mount Hood National Forest, 65 miles (2 hours) east of Portland.

Recommended time: Early September.

Minimum time commitment: 2 hours, plus driving time.

What to bring: Sturdy hiking boots, hat, sunglasses, sunscreen, binoculars, camera with wide-angle lens, lunch, water. The weather is often warm and sunny at this time of year, but mountain weather can be fickle, so bring warm clothing along with your shorts and T-shirt.

Admission fee: A Trail Park Pass is required. You can buy a day pass for $3 or a season pass for $25 from Forest Service offices and many sporting goods stores.

Directions: From Hood River, drive south on Oregon Highway 35 for 23 miles and turn right (west) onto Forest Road 3512 (Cooper Spur Road) toward Cooper Spur Ski Area. Continue on FR 3512 for 9 miles to Tilly Jane Campground. From Portland, drive east on U.S. Highway 26 for 52 miles to the junction with OR 35. Go east on OR 35 for 15 miles. Turn left (west) onto FR 3512. The upper portion of this road can be rough, but it is passable with regular-clearance vehicles if you drive with care.

The background: At 11,235 feet, Mount Hood is Oregon's tallest peak. It is a popular destination for mountain climbers, and thousands of people flock to its slopes every year to ascend its summit. Depending on the route taken, an ascent of Mount Hood often means crossing one of its 11 glaciers. These great permanent fields of ice gracing the mountain slopes are formed by snow that accumulates faster than it melts. They are potentially dangerous places of deep crevasses and ice cliffs that may crumble at any moment. Only well-trained and experienced mountaineers can safely travel across them.

But the nonclimber can get a bird's-eye view of one of these rivers of ice and the spectacular alpine landscape in which they are found from a ridgetop trail overlooking the Eliot Glacier on Mount Hood's north side. In the fall,

Cooper Spur, Mount Hood National Forest

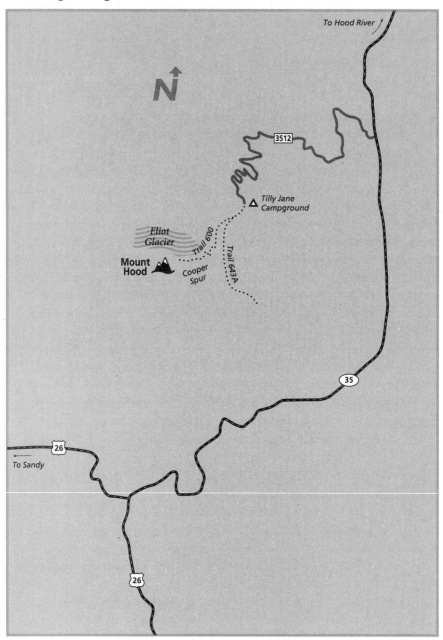

This massive glacier sprawls across the north flank of Mount Hood, astounding hikers along Cooper Spur.

the snow from the previous winter has finally melted away, revealing the sculptured terrain of the glacier's icy surface.

The fun: Park at Tilly Jane Campground and take Cooper Spur–Tilly Jane Trail (Trail 643A), which begins across a small stream at the campground's south end. Shortly, you will come to a turnoff on the right onto Cloud Cap Saddle Trail (Trail 600). Take that trail. It is 0.25 mile to the top of the ridge called Cooper Spur. The trail is a bit steep, but switchbacks make it a little easier. Once on the ridge, you are at an elevation of 8,514 feet. From here, you can hike along the top of the ridge toward the mountain as far as you care to walk. Eliot Glacier is below and to the south. The farther up the ridge you hike, the better your view of the glacier will be. The ridge is several miles long.

Do not climb down onto the glacier or attempt to climb to the summit of Mount Hood unless you and your companions are experienced mountaineers and have brought along all the necessary equipment.

Food and lodging: All services are available in Hood River and the community of Mount Hood. There is a campground located at the trailhead.

Next best: The drive on US 26 along Mount Hood offers many excellent views of the mountain. If you are looking for some close views of Oregon's highest peak but do not want to drive all the way around to the north side, stop at Timberline Lodge, from which you can get grand views of Mount Hood's south face. The road to Timberline Lodge is on the north side of US 26 about 27 miles east of Sandy.

For more information:

Mount Hood National Forest

Hood River Ranger District

6780 Highway 35

Parkdale, OR 97041

541-352-6002

Rivers of Ice

Glaciers are often described as rivers of ice, an analogy that is easy to understand when looking down upon one from above as it appears to flow down the mountainside. There are two basic types of glaciers: continental glaciers and valley glaciers. As you might assume, continental glaciers covered vast expanses of the earth. Originating in the northern polar areas, these great sheets of ice spread southward during the Pleistocene epoch, or the Ice Age, which lasted about 1 million years and ended some 10,000 years ago. During this time, about 32 percent of the earth's surface was covered with ice. As these glaciers advanced, they gouged rifts and depressions in the earth that would become valleys and lakes as the glaciers melted and receded. The only continental glaciers left on the planet today are in Greenland and Antarctica.

Valley glaciers, on the other hand, are relatively common in mountainous areas of the world, where they form from snowpack that accumulates faster than it melts. Because they are located on mountain slopes, over the centuries they slowly move downward, digging out a swath in the earth before them and depositing ridges on either side. These ridges are known as moraines.

The valley glaciers gracing the slopes of a large mountain can contain tremendous amounts of ice. The 11 glaciers on Mount Hood contain a total volume of over 12 billion cubic feet of snow and ice. That represents enough water to keep the Columbia River flowing for a full 18 hours.

Today, about 10 percent of the earth's surface is covered with glaciers and other ice. ∎

Grand Views
in a Big Country

28

Fall in Oregon's big sky country features aspens in golden splendor, grand vistas, and a taste of the freedom of the open range.

Site: Steens Mountain, 65 miles (1.5 hours) south of Burns.

Recommended time: Mid-September.

Minimum time commitment: 1 weekend.

What to bring: Camping gear, food, water, warm clothing, bird identification guide, spotting scope or binoculars, camera and wide-angle lens.

Admission fee: None.

Directions: From Burns, travel east on Oregon Highway 78 for 2 miles. Turn right (south) onto OR 205. Drive 60 miles to Frenchglen. Turn left (east) onto the dirt road at the south end of town, toward Page Springs Campground and Camper Corral (a commercial campground). Go 3.5 miles to the campground turnoff on the right. The gate that marks the beginning of the Steens Mountain Loop Road is just beyond.

The background: At 9,773 feet above sea level, Steens Mountain is a massive, 30-mile-long fault block mountain. Immense pressure deep within the earth's surface thrust it 1 vertical mile above the surrounding desert floor some 15 million years ago. Fourteen million years later, a series of Ice Age glaciers carved four 0.5-mile-deep, U-shaped gorges—Wildhorse, Little Indian, Big Indian, and Kiger—through the mountain. Sage-covered slopes, streams and springs, aspen groves, and mountain lakes add to Steens Mountain's spectacular beauty. Wildlife on the mountain includes elk, mule deer, bighorn sheep, pronghorn antelope, and hawks and eagles.

A 66-mile loop road begins near Page Springs Campground and ends on OR 205 about 7 miles south of Frenchglen. Because of heavy winter snowfall on Steens Mountain, the road usually is not open until early July and generally closes by the end of October.

Steens Mountain encompasses about 700,000 acres. Around 470,000 of those acres are managed by the Bureau of Land Management, while the remainder is privately owned.

The fun: Take the Steens Mountain Loop Road from Frenchglen as it gradually climbs up the less-steep west side, through grasslands and juniper forest. The road is gravel and rough in some places, and you may even encounter patches of snow to drive through or around. But the road is generally in fairly

Spectacular, glacier-carved gorges make Steens Mountain one of the most striking landscapes in the state.

good shape and passable with a passenger car if you drive slowly and carefully. There are some winding sections along the way, with steep drop-offs and no guardrails, so drive carefully.

As you ascend the mountain, you will pass through open grasslands and large groves of aspens. A good place to stop for your first look at one of the mountain's glacier-carved valleys is at the Kiger Gorge Overlook, at milepost 25. There is a parking lot there and a short trail to several viewpoints overlooking the gorge. This is also a prime spot to watch for mule deer and elk, as well as hawks and eagles, which like to soar on the thermal winds prevalent on the mountain. Three miles beyond is the East Rim Overlook. Stop in the parking area and walk over to the rim for a spectacular view of the mountain's steep east face and the Alvord Desert shimmering in the distance. Take a few minutes to scan the slopes and rock outcroppings here for bighorn sheep.

There are a total of eight viewpoints along the Loop Road before it descends back into the low sagebrush country.

Food and lodging: All services are available in Burns. Rooms are available at the Frenchglen Hotel in Frenchglen, but it is a good idea to make reservations in advance. There is also a restaurant in town. There are BLM campgrounds on Steens Mountain at Page Springs, Fish Lake, and Jackman Park. There is also a commercial RV campground, Camper Corral, just west of Page Springs.

Next best: If the Alvord Desert looks tantalizing to you, and if you have some extra time, pay it a visit. From Frenchglen, go south on OR 205 for about 50 miles to the junction with the Fields–Denio Road. Turn north and drive for about 6 miles. The Alvord Desert, which is actually a large, dry lakebed that periodically has water in it, is along the road to the east.

For more information:
Bureau of Land Management
Burns District
HC-74-12533
Highway 20 West
Hines, OR 97738
541-573-4400

Elk in Love

Watch bull Roosevelt elk gather in open meadows to bugle and battle as the fall rut, or mating season, swings into full heat.

Site: Jewell Meadows Wildlife Area, 60 miles (1.5 hours) northwest of Portland.

Recommended time: Mid- to late September.

Minimum time commitment: 2 hours, plus driving time.

What to bring: Binoculars or spotting scope, tape recorder.

Admission fee: None.

Directions: From Portland, take U.S. Highway 26 West and drive about 50 miles. Take the Jewell Junction exit, go right at the stop sign, and follow the signs to Jewell on Fishhawk Falls Highway for 8.7 miles. At the junction with Oregon Highway 202, turn left and drive 1.3 miles to the main office and viewing area.

The background: A herd of 280 to 300 Roosevelt elk wanders the forests, abandoned orchards, wetlands, and meadows of the 1,200-acre Jewell Meadows Wildlife Area. The Oregon Department of Fish and Wildlife manages the area in three separate parcels in the Humbug, Beneke, and Fishhawk Valleys to provide a source of food for the elk during the winter, as well as habitat for a variety of other native wildlife. Some parts of the wildlife area are tilled and seeded with hay crops to provide additional forage for the elk. The Department of Fish and Wildlife also maintains agreements with some adjacent landowners to provide a protective buffer zone around parts of the refuge.

During the autumn rut, the bugle of the bull elk reverberates through the forests and pastures of Jewell Meadows Wildlife Area.

Roosevelt elk can grow to a total weight of 700 to 1,000 pounds. Since 1972, about 1,500 elk from Jewell Meadows Wildlife Area have been trapped and transplanted to Oregon's Coast and Cascade Ranges, as well as to wilderness homes in California and Alaska.

During September and October, the elk breeding season is in full swing, peaking from mid- to late September. With it comes the opportunity to hear and see the big bulls bugling challenges to all comers as they collect a harem of cows to mate with.

The fun: The best bet is to start at the developed parking and viewing area by the wildlife area headquarters. Restrooms, an interpretive kiosk, and brochures about the area are available there. From the parking area, there is an expansive view south and west across the meadow next to Fishhawk Creek, where elk congregate. Beyond the meadow is dense forest. Scan the surrounding area for bull activity. Listen carefully for bugling. The long, high-pitched whistle is beautiful to hear and will help you zero in on the elk's location. If you are really lucky, you may even see two bulls sparring in an epic battle for dominance.

There are three other roadside viewing areas along OR 202. One is just before the headquarters and main parking lot, while the others are farther up the road. You may also see elk along Beneke Creek Road, which you can access by turning north off OR 202, just west of its junction with Fishhawk Falls Highway.

Food and lodging: The closest food, gas, and groceries are in Jewell Junction at the junction of US 26 and Fishhawk Falls Highway, 8.7 miles south of Jewell. The nearest town with all services is Astoria, 28 miles north on OR 202.

Next best: You may also see elk on a regular basis in the meadows along Fishhawk Creek, from December through mid-March. It is also possible to see cow elk and their calves beginning in mid-June.

For more information:

Jewell Meadows Wildlife Area
Oregon Department of Fish and Wildlife
HCR 60, Box 1565
Seaside, OR 97138
503-755-2264

Wilderness Whistlers

Some would say there is no more haunting sound in nature than the bugle of a bull elk in autumn. It begins as a bellow, becomes a shrill whistle, and ends with a series of grunts. From a distance, only the whistle can be heard as it echoes through the surrounding mountains and forest. When you hear it, you know that the elk rut, or mating season, has begun.

From August through November, adult bull elk join herds of cow elk, collecting harems and rounding up any cows that stray too far. They threaten rivals by bugling, rolling in pools of water and mud, and urinating on vegetation, which they toss over their backs with their antlers. If one bull challenges another for his cows, the battle is on. The bulls joust with their large racks of antlers, sometimes clashing violently, though injuries and death are rare. They duel until one gives up and retreats to the forest, while the winner claims or reclaims the harem. These fights for dominance may last hours or minutes, and a bull may collect up to 60 cows over the course of the rut.

In the early spring, the cows wander away from the herd to give birth to one or two calves that typically weigh 25 to 40 pounds. After about a week, they return to their herds with offspring in tow.

There are two subspecies of elk living in Oregon: Roosevelt elk on the west side of the Cascade Mountains and Rocky Mountain elk on the east side. ■

Kokanee on Parade

Thousands of bright red kokanee salmon migrate from Lake Billy Chinook up the Metolius River to spawn. They are easily seen at close range in the crystal-clear river water.

Site: Metolius River, 16 miles (25 minutes) northwest of Sisters.

Recommended time: Late September.

Minimum time commitment: 1 hour, plus driving time.

What to bring: Polarized sunglasses to help cut glare on the water surface, camera with telephoto lens and polarizing filter.

Admission fee: None.

Directions: From Sisters, take U.S. Highway 20 west and drive 9 miles. Turn right (north) onto Forest Road 14 at the sign for Camp Sherman. Drive 5 miles to Camp Sherman (turning right at the stop sign). After crossing the Metolius River at the Camp Sherman Store, bear left and continue on for 1.5 miles. Turn left at the turnoff for the Allingham Guard Station (FR 1217). Park on your left just over the bridge on the west side of the river.

The background: Fed by springs emanating from deep within the Cascade Mountains, the Metolius River rises fully formed just a couple of miles south of Camp Sherman. Lined with ponderosa pines, firs, and cedars, it flows about 30 miles to Lake Billy Chinook, home to a large population of kokanee salmon.

A popular game fish native to the Pacific Northwest, the kokanee is actually a type of landlocked sockeye salmon. Unable to reach the ocean, Lake Billy Chinook's kokanee instead spend their adult lives in the lake, migrating up the Metolius River in the fall in search of gravel beds in which to build nests and lay eggs. After spawning, the fish die, providing food for a variety of animals and returning nutrients to the earth as they decompose.

The fun: From the parking area at Allingham Bridge, follow a small riverside path for about 30 feet to where a small spring-fed stream enters the main river. Kokanee congregate here before swimming up the creek to spawn. For a close look at the spawning fish, walk up the creek. It flows through an open meadow and is only around 150 feet long.

The fish spawn all along the creek, including at the point where it originates from underground springs. You will see dead fish along the bank, many partially eaten by local wildlife, including minks, otters, and bears. The more dead fish there are along the bank and the fewer spawning fish in

Kokanee salmon ascend the Metolius River from Lake Billy Chinook each fall to spawn.

the creek, the later it is in the spawning process.

Kokanee actually spawn in many places along the Metolius River. If you have time, it is fun to walk along the riverbank and see if you can find other spawning areas.

Food and lodging: All services are available in Sisters. A small general store in Camp Sherman has groceries and fishing tackle. There are 10 Forest Service campgrounds along the river.

Next best: There is a fish observation deck and interpretive exhibit overlooking the Metolius River by the bridge at Camp Sherman. In the fall, you may see kokanee there. Throughout the year, you may see large rainbow trout swimming near and underneath the bridge.

For more information:

Deschutes National Forest
Sisters Ranger District
Pine Street and U.S. Highway 20
Sisters, OR 97759
541-549-2111

Raptors on the Wing³¹

Over 2,000 hawks and eagles pass along a 35-mile ridge in the Mount Hood National Forest as they migrate south in the fall. You can watch what is believed to be the largest concentration of migrating raptors in the state from the vantage of 5,600-foot Bonney Butte.

Site: Bonney Butte, 70 miles (2 hours) southeast of Portland.

Recommended time: Early October.

Minimum time commitment: 1 day.

What to bring: Binoculars with wide-angle field of view, bird or raptor identification guide, picnic lunch, blanket or folding chair.

Admission fee: None.

Directions: From Portland, drive about 52 miles southeast on U.S. Highway 26 to the junction with Oregon Highway 35. Head east on OR 35 for 4 miles and turn right (south) onto Forest Road 48 (White River Road). Drive 7 miles and then turn left onto FR 4890. Drive 3.75 miles, turn left onto FR 4891, and drive 4 miles to Bonney Meadows Campground. FR 4891 is a bit rough, but it is passable with a regular-clearance passenger vehicle if you are careful.

The background: As many as 2,500 migrating raptors follow the updrafts caused by a 35-mile-long, north-to-south-trending ridge just south of Mount Hood as they pass by during the fall on their way south for the winter. On a good day, over 200 raptors may fly by, including golden eagles, sharp-shinned hawks, Cooper's hawks, red-tailed hawks, and turkey vultures.

Because this is the busiest hawk migration corridor known in Oregon, the conservation organization HawkWatch International sets up an observation station here each fall to count and band these winged passersby. The information they gather is used to monitor the overall health of hawk populations.

The fun: Park at Bonney Meadows Campground and hike up the 0.75-mile spur road, which begins just a short walk north of the campground. It leads to the summit of Bonney Butte, where you can set up your chair or picnic and begin your hawk watch. The best way to find migrating hawks is to sweep the sky in a systematic pattern with your binoculars, aiming particularly toward the north, the direction from which most birds will appear. As you swing your binoculars back and forth, do not forget to occasionally look to the sides and overhead as well, because the hawks may be anywhere. As the day warms, thermal updrafts will cause the hawks to fly higher in the sky. During the cooler hours of early morning and late afternoon, the hawks fly lower.

HawkWatch International maintains a hawk watch station on Bonney Butte where staff members count and band birds. HawkWatch asks that you do not hike over to the station unless the station leader invites you.

Food and lodging: Food, lodging, and groceries are available about 16 miles east of Sandy, in the vicinity of Welches, Rhododendron, and Zigzag. All services are available in Sandy. On Bonney Butte, there is a campground for tents and trailers no longer than 22 feet.

Next best: Although the peak migration tends to be in early October, hawks pass through the area from mid-September through mid-October.

For more information:

HawkWatch International
P.O. Box 660
Salt Lake City, UT 84110
801-524-8511

The Long Journey Home

Watch salmon spawn along the banks of the Sandy River beneath a canopy of fall colors, just a short drive from Portland.

Site: Oxbow Regional Park, 25 miles (40 minutes) east of Portland.

Recommended time: Mid-October.

Minimum time commitment: 1 day.

What to bring: Sunglasses with polarizing lenses to cut glare on the water when viewing salmon, camera with telephoto lens and polarizing filter.

Admission fee: $3 per vehicle.

Directions: From Portland, drive east on Interstate 84 for 13 miles to exit 17 for Troutdale. Take this exit, pass the truck stop, and turn right onto 257th Avenue. Go 2.8 miles and turn left onto Southeast Division Street. Stay on Southeast Division Street (which eventually becomes Southeast Oxbow Road) for 4.8 miles. Then turn left onto Southeast Oxbow Parkway and drive 3.7 miles to the park.

The background: From late summer through October, spawning chinook salmon return from the ocean, where they grew to adulthood, to the Sandy

Oxbow Regional Park

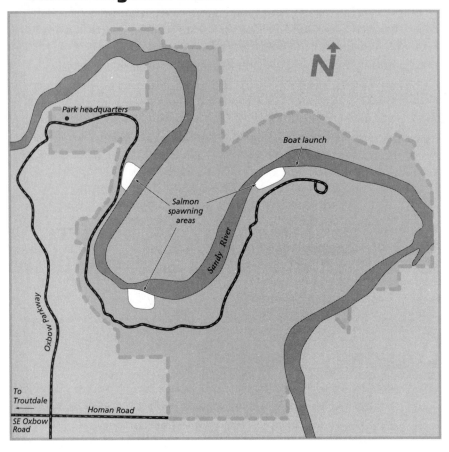

River in Oxbow Regional Park, where they were born four or five years earlier. Upon their arrival, they seek out regular spawning sites in the shallow, rocky riffles of the river. Females battle one another for prime locations to build nests and lay eggs, while males fight among themselves for the right to mate. In time, the females build their redds, or nests, by wriggling out a depression in the stream bottom. Then the males and females deposit eggs and milt, which are mixed together by the moving current and buried with gravel. Next spring, when the young salmon emerge from the gravel, their parents will have been long dead, exhausted from their arduous journey from the sea, the rigors of spawning, and the lack of food. After a year or two in the Sandy River, these young fish will migrate to the ocean, to return one day just as their parents did and begin the cycle anew.

The fun: Attend the Salmon Festival held on the second weekend in October. There are a variety of booths featuring different conservation organizations, salmon experts to answer your questions about these remarkable fish, live music, and food. Park naturalists lead free salmon walks along the river to active spawning grounds.

If you want to explore on your own, a trail leads along much of the river's south bank. It is best to check first with park staff (at the headquarters building on the right immediately as you enter the park) for up-to-date information on spawning activity. Periodic flooding moves gravel around in the river, altering the location of some spawning grounds and eliminating others. One still-active site is just downstream from the boat launch, 2.1 miles up the park road from headquarters. Maps of the park and spawning grounds are available at park headquarters.

Food and lodging: Food and lodging is available along I-84 off exit 17.

Next best: If you cannot make the Salmon Festival, you can see the salmon spawning throughout October. Park staff members lead guided salmon-watching trips every weekend during the month.

For more information:

Oxbow Regional Park
3010 SE Oxbow Parkway
Gresham, OR 97080
503-663-4708

Chinook salmon spawn new generations and an annual festival along the banks of the Sandy River in Oxbow Regional Park.

Journey of the Salmon

The life cycle of the salmon is one of nature's most mysterious wonders. Each year, these fish emerge from the Pacific Ocean and make their way up the streams and rivers of Oregon to reach the waters in which they were born—to spawn there and then die.

Salmon species in Oregon include chinook, coho, sockeye, and chum, along with steelhead, a seagoing rainbow trout. Some types of cutthroat trout also spend part of their lives in the ocean. These fish are *anadromous*, which means they are born in freshwater, live their adult lives in the ocean, and then return to freshwater to mate and lay eggs.

The cycle of the salmon begins (and ends) in a freshwater stream or river. Hatching from eggs laid in gravel on the stream bottom as much as four months earlier, the fry emerge in the spring. Depending on the species, these young fish may head for the ocean immediately or remain in the stream for several years. Chum salmon fry go right to sea, for example, while sockeye spend up to three years in freshwater before migrating to the ocean. Steelhead and cutthroat trout remain in freshwater for up to four years, while coho salmon stay for up to two years. Chinook salmon are the most variable; young chinooks stay in their natal stream anywhere from three months to two years, depending on whether they are fall or spring migrating fish, respectively. As the fish migrate to the ocean, they undergo a change in their body chemistry that adapts them to life

in saltwater. This is called *smoltification*, and young salmon on their way to the ocean are called *smolts*.

Once in the ocean, each species inhabits a specific area. Chum and sockeye salmon migrate to the Gulf of Alaska. Chinook salmon tend to spread out from the Gulf of Alaska to northern California, while coho salmon stay just off the Oregon coast. The whereabouts of others during this stage of life— among them steelhead and some populations of chinook—remain a mystery.

Spending anywhere from one to four years at sea, the fish feed on plankton, shrimp, and other fish and grow prodigiously. Chinook salmon have been known to top 100 pounds. Coho salmon average 6 to 12 pounds, sockeye around 4 to 8 pounds, chum 6 pounds, and steelhead around 5 to 15 pounds.

After living in the ocean for one to four years, the adult fish begin returning to their home rivers to spawn, finding their way across thousands of miles of trackless saltwater. The timing of spawning migrations varies from species to species and even within some species. Coho and chum salmon return each fall. Sockeye return in summer. Steelhead have summer and winter spawning runs, while chinook return in separate spring, summer, and fall migrations. Along the way, the migrating fish run a gauntlet of predators, including humans.

Upon reaching the exact location in

the stream where they were born, the females begin digging nests, called *redds*, in the stream bottom by making sideways motions of their bodies, while males jostle with one another for the right to mate. As the females begin to lay eggs, the males join them, depositing sperm at the same time. The females each build a number of nests, lay eggs, and defend their redds until they, along with the males, die about a week later. Their bodies provide nourishment for the many scavengers that feast on them.

Although death pervades the end of a salmon spawning run, thousands of eggs lie beneath the gravel. From these will emerge a new generation of these great fish, and the cycle of the salmon will begin anew. ■

The Hues of Autumn  33

This 36-mile drive shimmers with the reds and yellows of fall colors while offering expansive vistas of the Cascade Mountains.

Site: Oregon Highway 242 (McKenzie Highway), from the junction of U.S. Highway 126 to Sisters.

Recommended time: Late October. Because fall colors may peak at different times from year to year, it is recommended that you call the contact numbers listed below for the latest fall foliage update.

Minimum time commitment: 2 to 5 hours, depending upon how often you stop to take in the views or walk the trails.

What to bring: Camera, binoculars, warm jacket or windbreaker, hiking boots.

Admission fee: Trail Park Passes are required at trailheads along this route. You can buy a day pass for $3 or a season pass for $25 from Forest Service offices and many sporting goods stores.

Directions: To reach the junction of US 126 and OR 242, go east from Eugene on US 126 for 50 miles. On the east side of the mountains, OR 242 can be accessed off US 20 in the town of Sisters, 18 miles northwest of Bend.

The background: A designated Oregon Scenic Byway, the 36-mile long McKenzie Highway climbs over the crest of the Cascade Mountains. It passes through deep forest and over the summit of 5,325-foot McKenzie Pass, roughly following the route of an 1860s wagon road.

The dry east slope of the mountains is cloaked in ponderosa pines, which give way to firs and spruces at the higher elevations. On the summit of the pass, you will be treated to spectacular views of the peaks known as Three Sisters to the south, and Mount Washington, Mount Jefferson, and Three Fingered Jack to the north across a vast lava field. The lava fields in this part of Oregon are stark reminders of the area's fiery, volcanic past. Some of them are the result of volcanic eruptions that occurred as recently as 400 years ago.

On the western slope, you will find a dense forest of Douglas-firs that is typical of the wetter climate that prevails there. Beneath this canopy is a profusion of vine maples, which turn bright red as cool autumn temperatures arrive.

There are also many lakes and trails along the route, offering plenty of opportunities to get out of your car and experience autumn in the mountains firsthand.

The fun: Although you can begin this trip from either side of the mountains, most people start on the west side, where the fall colors are best.

A good place to make your first stop is at Proxy Falls, about 9 miles from the junction of US 126 and OR 242. An easy 1-mile trail leads to Upper and Lower Proxy Falls through a lava field dotted with bright-red vine maples. There is a restroom at the trailhead parking area.

From there, continue east. The highway becomes very narrow and winding, necessitating slow, cautious driving. It is along this stretch up Deadhorse Grade (which climbs 1,200 feet in 4 miles) where the best fall colors can be seen in the red hues of vine maples and the yellows of bigleaf maples. About 8 miles from the falls, you will come to the Hand Lake Trailhead on the north side of the road. This is an easy 0.5-mile walk to a large meadow.

About 5 miles beyond that is the summit of McKenzie Pass. Stop at the parking area and climb the stone stairway to the Dee Wright Observatory. This structure, constructed from lava rock, has windows that offer framed views of the major peaks of the central Oregon Cascades. The mountain panorama here is nothing less than awesome. Take 15 minutes or so to hike the paved 0.5-mile Lava Loop Trail, complete with interpretive signs describing the many volcanic features to be found here. The trailhead is immediately east of the observatory. There are restrooms just to the west.

As you continue down the eastern slope, be sure to stop at Cold Springs Campground (about 10 miles from the summit), with its dense stands of colorful aspens, and walk the short trail along the springs immediately to the left as you turn into the parking area. Sisters, and the end of the highway tour, is another 5 miles down the road.

Food and lodging: There are no services along this stretch of highway. Food, lodging, and gas are available along OR 126 west of the McKenzie Highway junction and in Sisters at the eastern terminus.

Next best: For your return trip, take US 20 west from Sisters over 4,817-foot high Santiam Pass to see more aspens and vine maples.

For more information:

Willamette National Forest
McKenzie Ranger District
57600 McKenzie Highway
McKenzie Bridge, OR 97413
541-822-3381

Deschutes National Forest
Sisters Ranger District
Pine Street and U.S. Highway 20
Sisters, OR 97759
541-549-2111

Going Underground 34

Visit the subterranean world of stalactites, stalagmites, bats, blind insects, and other strange sights at Oregon Caves National Monument.

Site: Oregon Caves National Monument, 47 miles (1 hour) south of Grants Pass.

Recommended time: Late October.

Minimum time commitment: 1 day.

What to bring: Sturdy footwear with slip-proof soles, camera with electronic flash and wide-angle lens. The cave maintains a year-round temperature of 40 degrees Fahrenheit, so warm clothes are a must if you plan to take the cave tour.

Admission fee: Cave tours are $7.50 for ages 12 and up, $5 for children 11 and under.

Directions: From Grants Pass, drive southwest on U.S. Highway 199 for 28 miles to Cave Junction. From there, follow Oregon Highway 46, a very winding road, 19 miles east to the national monument parking area.

The background: A 3-mile-long cave can be found deep inside the earth at this 480-acre national monument. Formed over 10,000 years ago, it contains stalactites, stalagmites, flowstone, cave popcorn, rimstone dams, moon milk, cave ghosts, clay worms, box work, cave pearls, soda straws, and other strange and eerie formations.

The fun: Take a guided tour through a 0.5-mile segment of the cave. Tours are offered on a daily basis from 10 A.M. to 4 P.M. at 1.5-hour intervals and include an informative lecture about the cave's history, ecology, and geology. Visitors wander the cave's narrow passageways on a lighted, mostly paved trail, discovering new underground wonders around each bend. The tour involves climbing or descending a total of 500 steps. Children must be at least 42 inches tall to go on the tour, which lasts about 75 minutes. You can purchase tour tickets at the gift shop.

Food and lodging: The Chateau, a lodge built in 1934 and located in the national monument, is generally open through late October. The restaurant is closed at this time of year, but the coffee shop is open and offers a limited menu. All services are available in Cave Junction. There are campgrounds in the surrounding Siskiyou National Forest.

Next best: If time is short, or you suffer from claustrophobia, there are a variety of trails through the national monument's old-growth forest that make for interesting hikes.

For more information:
Oregon Caves National Monument
19000 Caves Highway
Cave Junction, OR 97523
541-592-2100

Strange subterranean sights abound at Oregon Caves National Monument, south of Grants Pass.

The Making of Oregon Caves

About 220 million years ago, southwestern Oregon was an ocean basin filled with a variety of sea creatures. As they died and accumulated on the sea floor, their bodies formed calcite-rich mud, which later hardened into limestone.

As time went on, movement of the earth's crust uplifted the basin, creating land where there once was seawater. Heat and pressure caused by these rumblings in the earth baked the limestone into marble. The earth shook some more, grinding into the Siskiyou Mountains to the east, ripping and twisting cracks and faults into the layers of rock. Next, water began to seep through the ground, following faults and cracks in the rocks that offered paths of least resistance. Over time, this constant flow of water eroded rooms, chambers, and tunnels into the underground layer of marble—and Oregon Caves was born. By 10,000 years ago, the relentless seepage of water had carved an opening from the depths of the cave to the surface.

In the meantime, groundwater containing calcium carbonate draining into the cave created stalactites and stalagmites. Other underground formations in the cave include minuscule calcite crystals called moon milk; cave popcorn, a residue left behind when moist air blowing from outside the cave evaporated; and cave ghosts, small bumps that are all that remain of former stalagmites dissolved by acidified water dripping from the cave ceiling.

Although Oregon Caves is full of wonders, it was not discovered until 1874, when a hunter named Elijah Davidson followed his dog into a hole in the ground in pursuit of a bear. Once inside, Davidson realized he was in a cave and wandered deeper down the passageway, until the last of the matches he used to light his way was gone. He followed the stream that ran through the cave back out to daylight, with his dog close behind.

In 1907 the California poet Joaquin Miller visited Oregon Caves and was so taken with its beauty that he wrote a poem called "Marble Halls of Oregon." The publicity the poem garnered helped call attention to the need to preserve the area and, in 1909, President William Howard Taft designated 480 acres surrounding the cave as Oregon Caves National Monument. ■

See a record in the rocks from a time when Oregon was a steamy jungle full of strange creatures at a place renowned for its fossils and geologic features.

Site: John Day Fossil Beds National Monument, 80 miles (1.5 hours) east of Prineville.

Recommended time: Late October.

Minimum time commitment: 1 day.

What to bring: Geology guide (available at the visitor center), camera, water, picnic lunch, sun hat, sunglasses, sunscreen, sturdy hiking boots for walking rock-strewn paths.

Admission fee: None.

Directions: Travel 77 miles east from Prineville on U.S. Highway 26. Then turn left (north) onto Oregon Highway 19 and go 2 miles to the visitor center in the Sheep Rock Unit. To reach the Clarno Unit, continue north on OR 19 for 64 miles to Fossil. Turn left (west) onto OR 218 and drive 20 miles. The Painted Hills Unit is 6 miles north of US 26 off Bridge Creek Road, 42 miles east of Prineville.

The background: Forty million years of eastern Oregon history are preserved in the rock formations in what is one of the richest fossil deposits in North America. Although this part of Oregon is desert today, in the distant past it harbored woodlands, savannas, and jungles, which were inhabited by camels, horses, sloths, bears, peccaries, rhinoceroses, and even an early form of elephant.

The national monument is divided into three separate units: Sheep Rock, Painted Hills, and Clarno. They encompass a total of 14,000 acres. Each unit tells its own unique story, imbedded in the rocks for all who take the time to look.

The headquarters and visitor center are located in the Sheep Rock Unit, where you can browse the small museum, attend an interpretive lecture, or pick up maps, books, and other information on the area's geology and prehistoric life in the bookstore. The Clarno Unit features a spectacular set of cliffs called the Clarno Palisades. A trail runs along their base. The most striking unit is the Painted Hills, where erosion of volcanic ash has created striking shades of pink, bronze, tan, black, and red on the hillsides.

John Day Fossil Beds National Monument, Sheep Rock Unit

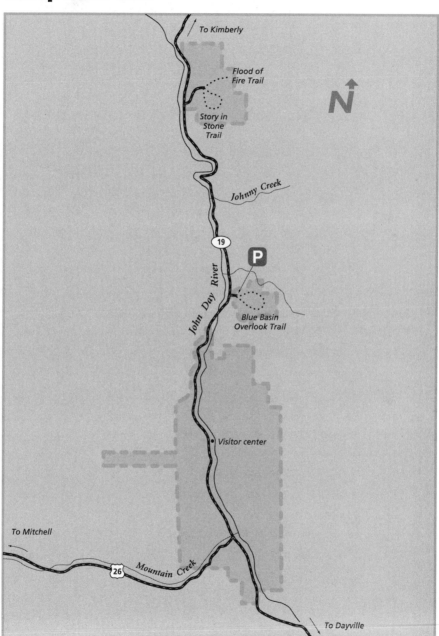

John Day Fossil Beds National Monument, Clarno Unit

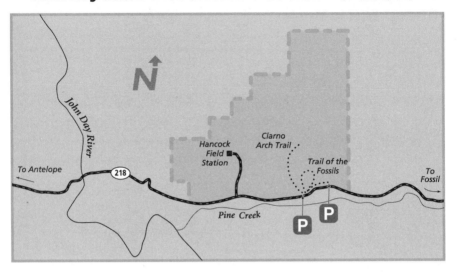

John Day Fossil Beds National Monument, Painted Hills Unit

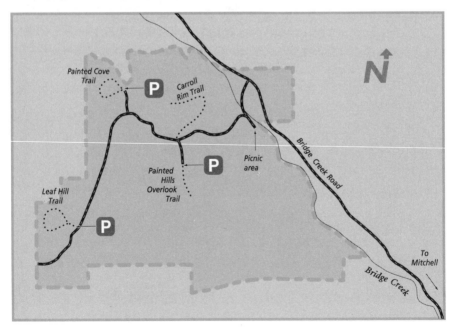

A hike through the geologic wonderland of John Day Fossil Beds National Monument reveals 40 million years' worth of Oregon history.

There are trails at each unit, allowing visitors a close look at various geologic formations.

The fun: If you have a full day, take in each unit starting with the Painted Hills. Hike Painted Hills Overlook Trail, 0.5-mile round-trip, for great views. Then stop at the visitor center in the Sheep Rock Unit to hear a lecture, see the museum, and pick up maps and brochures. Stop at the Foree Area, just up the road, for a picnic and hike on either the Flood of Fire or Story in Stone interpretive trail. Both are 0.25 mile, round-trip. At the Clarno Unit, the Trail of Fossils, 0.25-mile round-trip, takes you along spectacular cliffs imprinted with fossil leaves from a prehistoric forest.

Food and lodging: All services are available in Prineville and Dayville.

Next best: For a shorter trip involving considerably less driving, visit the Painted Hills Unit—easily the most spectacular of the three—and then stop at the Sheep Rock Unit for a picnic lunch on the grounds of the visitor center.

For more information:
John Day Fossil Beds National Monument
HCR 82, Box 126
Kimberly, OR 97848
541-987-2333

Changing Weather

Although much of the area in the vicinity of John Day Fossil Beds National Monument is desert and rangeland today, over the course of millions of years it has actually undergone many changes in climate and topography. Scientists know so much about the area's past because of the well-preserved layers of rocks found here. If you know how to read the layers, they tell a fascinating story of climatic evolution and its effect on the terrain and the animals that lived here through the eons.

From 37 to 54 million years ago, strange creatures now extinct, with names like hyaenadont, amynodont, and brontotheres, roamed a tropical forest here along with the ancestors of cats, horses, and rhinoceroses. Scientists know that the climate was warm and moist then because fossils from this time period are rich in the leaves, branches, nuts, roots, and fruits of plants from tropical and subtropical forests.

About 20 million years ago the climate changed, and the area became drier and cooler. Deciduous forest replaced the lush tropical one. Fossils of dogs, cats, horses, rhinoceroses, rodents, camels, and pigs are found in the rock layers from this time period.

Around 15 million years ago, volcanic eruptions and flows of molten lava covered the region numerous times, destroying the forests and adding a level layer of volcanic rock over the top of the earth's surface. The combination of a relatively moderate climate, layers of ash, and regular rainfall created fertile soils that encouraged a mix of deciduous forest and grassland. The animals that lived on the open grasslands included deer, dogs, cats, weasels, camels, horses, and bears.

Rock strata laid down 6 to 8 million years ago indicate that the climate had grown drier and cooler. There are fewer fossils in this layer, as the area came to be dominated by grassland.

Today much of this country is dry and open and populated by deer, antelope, and other typical animals of western rangelands. But the record in the rocks tells us that this is only a temporary state, and slowly and inexorably, changes will come once again to the John Day country. ▪

The Working Forest

It is a fact that humans depend heavily on forests for the wood products used to make building materials, paper, and other necessities of life. See how professional foresters manage woodlands to provide wood fiber for a growing population.

Site: Intensive Management Demonstration Trail, Peavy Arboretum, 5 miles (10 minutes) north of Corvallis.

Recommended time: Early November.

Minimum time commitment: 2 hours, plus driving time.

What to bring: Hiking boots, field guide to trees and shrubs.

Admission fee: None.

Directions: Drive north from Corvallis on Oregon Highway 99W for 4 miles. Turn left (west) onto Peavy Arboretum Road. The entrance to the arboretum is 0.7 mile on the left. Bear left at the first intersection, then right at the next, and continue a short distance to the trailhead parking lot.

The background: Peavy Arboretum is part of the 7,000-acre McDonald Research Forest, which is owned by Oregon State University and managed for timber and other natural resources. A variety of ongoing research projects are conducted here, some of which date back to the early 1920s.

The research goal of this "living laboratory" is to learn more about the ecological relationships found within forests, allowing foresters to balance the needs of a healthy forest with techniques to maximize the benefits of forests for humans. Intensive forest management means using a variety of methods, such as planting trees, thinning and pruning, controling weeds, and fertilizing, to produce high-quality wood in as short a time as possible.

Peavy Arboretum has a collection of over 200 species of trees and shrubs from throughout the world, which can be viewed from four trails within the immediate vicinity, as well as additional trails throughout the entire forest.

The fun: An easy 1.25-mile walk, the Intensive Management Demonstration Trail begins at the north end of the parking area and leads through a variety of forest types. There are 13 interpretive signs along the way that explain the forest management techniques and activities that have been utilized here. Pick up a trail-guide brochure at the trailhead. It explains in detail the sights you will see along your walk.

Food and lodging: All services are available in Corvallis.

Next best: Other trails at the arboretum include the Forest Discovery Trail, the Woodland Trail, and a trail to the Firefighter Memorial Shelter. You can pick up brochures on these trails as well as brochures on the arboretum and McDonald Forest at the Badewitz Kiosk. To reach the kiosk, drive 0.3 mile from the arboretum entrance, following the signs to the forest research office.

For more information:
Peavy Arboretum
8692 Peavy Arboretum Road
Corvallis, OR 97330
541-737-4452

Shifting Sands

Winter storms sculpt massive dunes, some exceeding 400 feet high, that stretch for nearly 60 miles along the central Oregon coast.

Site: Umpqua Dunes Trail, Oregon Dunes National Recreation Area, 9 miles (10 minutes) south of Reedsport.

Recommended time: Mid-November.

Minimum time commitment: 1 to 4 hours, plus driving time.

What to bring: Rain gear, warm jacket, hat, gloves, lunch, water, waterproof hiking boots, binoculars, camera.

Admission fee: Purchase a $3-per-vehicle daily admission permit or a $25 annual permit at the Oregon Dunes National Recreation Area headquarters at the junction of U.S. Highway 101 and Oregon Highway 38 in Reedsport. There are also self-service permit pay stations at the trailhead parking lot on South Jetty Road, 0.6 mile south of Florence, and at a number of other locations within the area.

Directions: Drive south from Reedsport on US 101 for 9 miles. Turn right (west) into the parking lot at the sign for the Umpqua Dunes Trail. After entering the parking area, bear to the right. The trail begins at the bridge over Eel Creek.

The background: A 56-mile stretch of rolling sand dunes was created along the central Oregon Coast about 7,000 years ago when sand eroded from hills and mountains and carried to the sea by rivers was redeposited back on shore by ocean currents. Winds blowing off the ocean played, and continue to play, a role as well, sculpting the sand into ever-changing shapes reminiscent of the

Anatomy of a Sand Dune

A walk across the shifting sands of Oregon Dunes National Recreation Area will quickly reveal that it is much more than piles of sand along the ocean. These dunes, shaped by wind, water, and even vegetation, have their own unique anatomy and terminology.

The dune landscape changes as you move inland from the sea. Sand on the ocean bottom just offshore—carried by currents, waves, and tides—constantly adds to the beach. Heavier, larger sand grains remain on the beach while lighter, smaller grains are blown inland by ocean winds to build sand dunes.

Inland from the beach is the foredune, a low hill of sand that runs parallel to the water's edge. In the early 1900s, an exotic plant called European beach grass was planted in the area to stabilize the dunes and keep them from moving. The roots of this grass anchor the sand, preventing normal dune-building activity and creating the foredune. Just behind the foredune are hummocks where sand collects around plants that grow in the sand.

As the foredune is built up, it forms a barrier that prevents more sand from being deposited just beyond it. Instead, the wind wears the ground surface down to the water table. So as you move inland, you find a low, wetland area full of water-loving plants and wildlife. This is called the deflation plain.

Beyond the deflation plain, the dunes begin. Here you will find three types of dunes: transverse, oblique, and parabola, in that order. S-shaped transverse dunes are formed by northwesterly summer winds and can get up to 20 feet high. Oblique dunes are among the largest in the recreation area, created by winter and summer winds. The shape of these dunes constantly shifts depending on which way the prevailing winds blow. Oblique dunes can grow to as much as 500 feet above sea level and reach a mile in length. Parabola dunes are formed when stiff winds coming from the ocean blow out unstable sections of forest along the coast. After the trees erode away, the wind creates a U-shaped swath of sand reaching into the forest. This is a parabola dune.

Interspersed among the dunes are tree islands, where isolated stands of evergreens are slowly being buried by encroaching sands. Beyond the dunes, farther inland, the forest becomes more dominant as the direct influence of the sand and the sea wanes, finally fading altogether as you enter the Coast Range and an ecosystem more influenced by rain than by wind. ▪

Sahara Desert. During the winter, south and southwesterly winds of up to 100 miles per hour move tons of sand, shape and reshape dunes and ridges, and even partially bury stands of trees exposed to the open sea.

Today, a 40-mile stretch of this coastline is under the jurisdiction of the Forest Service and managed as the Oregon Dunes National Recreation Area. In addition to the extensive sand dunes, you will find forests, wetlands, lakes, rivers, streams, and miles of beach.

The fun: Hike the Umpqua Dunes Trail. You have two choices: the 1-mile interpretive loop trail or the 5.5-mile round-trip trail to the beach.

For an educational experience, the interpretive loop trail (which passes through the adjacent Eel Creek Campground) has seven stations that describe the forces that have created this remarkable place. You will pass through coastal coniferous forest, dunes, and even some wetlands. A brochure available at the visitor center in Reedsport and at the trailhead guides you through the various stations. For the most part, the trail is well-packed, although there are some areas of loose sand in the southern section.

For a wilder experience, bear left at the intersection after crossing the Eel Creek bridge and hike out to the beach through the largest dunes on the coast.

Food and lodging: All services are available in Reedsport and Florence. There are campgrounds in the Dunes National Recreation Area.

Next best: If you would like to see the dunes but are not in the mood for a lot of walking, take the South Jetty Road, 0.6 mile south of Florence on the west side of US 101. The road runs along the beach, ending near the mouth of the Siuslaw River, and gives quick, easy access to the surrounding dunes. There is a self-service pay station 2.1 miles from the road's junction with the highway.

For more information:

Oregon Dunes National Recreation Area
Siuslaw National Forest
855 Highway 101
Reedsport, OR 97467
541-271-3611

Wetlands at Work

The 60 inches of rain that falls annually on the coastal forest seeps through the ground to replenish the wetlands and estuary below. Follow its course on a trail from forest to tidal flat.

Site: South Slough National Estuarine Research Reserve, 9 miles (15 minutes) west of Coos Bay.

Recommended time: Mid-November.

Minimum time commitment: 3 hours, plus driving time.

What to bring: Rain gear, waterproof hiking boots, binoculars, bird identification guide, lunch, water.

Admission fee: None.

Directions: From Coos Bay, drive southwest on the Cape Arago Highway for about 4 miles to the Charleston Boat Basin. Cross the bridge, go 0.3 mile, and turn left (south) onto Seven Devils Road. Drive 4.1 miles, turn left at the sign for the Estuarine Research Reserve, and continue 0.2 mile to the parking area.

The background: South Slough National Estuarine Research Reserve encompasses about 4,600 acres within the 19,000-acre South Slough watershed. Established in 1974, the reserve was set aside as a place to study estuaries, to educate people about the importance of estuaries, and to provide recreational opportunities to the public. It is managed jointly by the Oregon Division of State Lands and the National Oceanic and Atmospheric Administration. Across the nation, there are currently 22 national estuarine research reserves.

South Slough National Estuarine Research Reserve has nearly 4,000 acres of forest lands and an additional 600 acres of tidal lands, including a substantial area of tidal flats. There is a laboratory on the reserve where staff scientists conduct research on marsh ecology, wetland restoration, and the impacts of nonnative, introduced species of plants and animals, among other things. There is a small interpretive center with exhibits. The reserve also offers a variety of educational programs and classes for children and adults.

A number of trails on the reserve take visitors to a variety of the South Slough watershed's habitats, including uplands, salt marsh, tidal flats, and open water channels.

The fun: The trail system emanating from the parking lot and visitor center offers access to coastal environments that are often difficult to reach along other parts of the Oregon Coast. The best route is the Hidden Creek Trail,

Where Saltwater and Freshwater Meet

Oregon's estuaries were created about 10,000 years ago when the last of the Ice Age glaciers melted, raising the ocean around 400 feet and flooding the mouths of such rivers as the Columbia, Tillamook, Umpqua, Yaquina, and Coos. Estuaries are, quite simply, the transition zone between saltwater and freshwater where rivers flow into the ocean.

Protected from the jarring force of waves that pound the beaches, estuaries are quiet places. And because nutrients, detritus, and other organic matter carried downriver and washed up from the ocean mingle here, estuaries are among the most biologically productive spots on the planet.

Because of the biological richness and protected nature of estuaries, they are important habitat for numerous fish species. Salmon, shad, and sturgeon rest here before migrating upstream to spawn. Some species of salmon live in estuaries during their juvenile life stage. Estuaries are also critical resting and staging areas for migrating waterfowl and shorebirds, which may gather at these areas by the thousands during the spring and fall.

There are actually five different habitats within an estuary: open water, eelgrass bed, mudflat, salt marsh, and upland. In the open water, you will find a variety of fish species, including chinook and coho salmon, along with seals, cormorants, and other animals that eat fish. Eelgrass beds are found next to open water areas and are only exposed during the lowest of tides. Here lurk Dungeness crabs, Pacific herring, shiner perch, bay pipefish, and black brant, a small species of goose. Mudflats, exposed at low tide, are smorgasbords for shorebirds. Under the mud dwell ghost shrimp, worms, clams, and pea crabs, which are eaten by great blue herons and other birds that patrol this habitat for tasty morsels. Salt marshes are found in the protected fringes of estuaries where pickleweed and salt grass grow and kingfishers dive into the water to catch sculpins, shiner perch, and baby salmon. Finally, away from the water are upland areas, above the high-tide zone. A variety of native and nonnative plants grow here, including yellow lupine, yarrow, Scotch broom, and European beach grass.

Unfortunately, the health of many estuaries—along with their biological richness—has been degraded by dredging, pollution, and human development. ■

which you can reach by following the sign to the right just as you enter the parking lot. Beginning at about the 200-foot elevation mark, the trail descends around 100 feet to hook up with Hidden Creek and then snakes about 1.5 miles to sea level and an observation platform. From there you can continue less than 0.25 mile to the estuary's edge, making for a round trip of just over 3 miles. The tidal flats and estuary are a great place to see wintering waterfowl and shorebirds. There is a restroom at the viewing platform.

Food and lodging: All services are located in Coos Bay.

Next best: For a shorter introduction to the reserve, take the Ten Minute Trail, which begins behind the visitor center. Although it does not approach the estuary, there is a viewpoint overlooking the watershed along the way. As its name implies, this 0.25-mile trail takes about 10 minutes to walk.

For more information:

South Slough National Estuarine Research Reserve
Oregon Division of State Lands
P.O. Box 5417
Charleston, OR 97420
541-888-5558

Shorebird Sanctuary 39

Millions of waterfowl and shorebirds—including ducks, geese, swans, and cranes—gather at this wetland along the Columbia River each winter.

Site: Sauvie Island Wildlife Area, 10 miles (20 minutes) northwest of Portland.

Recommended time: Late November.

Minimum time commitment: 3 hours, plus driving time.

What to bring: Rain gear, waterproof boots, spotting scope or binoculars, bird identification guide.

Admission fee: A parking pass is $3 a day or $10.50 a year. You may purchase one at the wildlife area headquarters and at Sam's Cracker Barrel Grocery on Sauvie Island, as well as at most sporting goods stores that sell hunting and fishing licenses.

Directions: From Portland, drive northwest on U.S. Highway 30 for 7.7 miles. Turn right and cross the Sauvie Island Bridge at the sign for the wildlife area.

Sauvie Island Wildlife Area

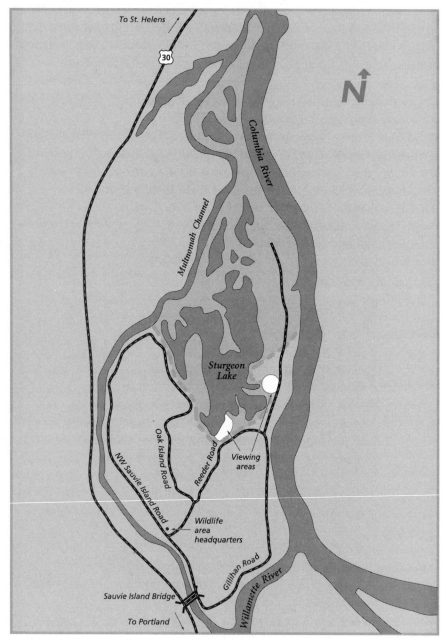

You are now on Northwest Sauvie Island Road. Continue west for 2 miles to the junction with Reeder Road. Bear right onto Reeder Road. The first viewing area is on the left in 3.1 miles. The second viewing area is on the left in 7 miles. The wildlife area headquarters is on the right-hand side of Northwest Sauvie Island Road, 0.2 mile past the junction with Reeder Road.

The background: Up to 3 million ducks and geese visit Sauvie Island Wildlife Area between October and April as they migrate down the Pacific Flyway. As many as 150,000 may be present at any given time. Some 2,000 tundra swans, an equal number of sandhill cranes, and huge numbers of Canada geese flock to this sanctuary of wetlands and croplands during the same period. Great blue herons are particularly common.

Managed by the Oregon Department of Fish and Wildlife especially for migrating waterfowl, the 12,000-acre Sauvie Island Wildlife Area is a mix of open water, streamside habitat, uplands, and farmlands. About 1,000 acres of the wildlife area are planted with buckwheat, millet, corn, and grain crops to provide green forage for ducks and geese during the fall.

Over 250 species of birds visit the wildlife area at some time during the course of the year. Twelve species of reptiles and amphibians and 37 species of mammals also make their home here, with black-tailed deer being the most frequently spotted.

Much of the wildlife area is closed during the fall and winter to prevent

Sturgeon Lake is a popular birding location at Sauvie Island Wildlife Area.

wintering birds from being disturbed. Closely regulated hunting is allowed.

The fun: Head for the first viewing area, 3.1 miles from the junction of Reeder and Northwest Sauvie Island Roads. There is an interpretive kiosk here and a short, paved trail up a gentle slope leading to expansive views of the southern end of Sturgeon Lake. You can set up a spotting scope here and scan the open water for a variety of waterfowl. It is not especially unusual to spot 100 great blue herons feeding on the lake.

The next viewing site, 3.9 miles farther down Reeder Road, will give you views along a canal and fields where waterfowl rest and feed.

Food and lodging: Groceries are available at Sam's Cracker Barrel Grocery on Sauvie Island near the bridge from the mainland. There is no gas available on the island. All services can be found in Portland, 10 miles to the southeast.

Next best: This is a good area in which to see bald eagles from January through March. They congregate here to prey on weak and injured ducks and geese.

For more information:

Sauvie Island Wildlife Area
18330 NW Sauvie Island Road
Portland, OR 97231
503-621-3488

Winter

Rainy Day
Rain Forest

A winter visit to this fog-shrouded headland reveals in all its glory a classic coastal forest of old-growth Sitka spruce.

Site: Giant Spruce Trail, Cape Perpetua Interpretive Center, 25 miles (20 minutes) south of Newport.

Recommended time: Early December.

Minimum time commitment: 3 hours, plus driving time.

What to bring: Rain gear, warm jacket, hat, gloves, water, trail snacks, waterproof hiking boots, camera.

Admission fee: $3 per vehicle.

Directions: From Newport, drive south on U.S. Highway 101 for 22.8 miles to Yachats. The entrance road to Cape Perpetua Interpretive Center is 2.5 miles south of Yachats on the left (east). Drive up the access road for 0.2 mile to the interpretive center parking area.

The background: The temperate rain forests of the Pacific Northwest coast are among the most spectacular in the world. Nurtured by fog and an annual rainfall that may exceed 100 inches per year, these forests are lush and dense with trees that live 1,000 years and grow to more than 200 feet tall.

Although coastal temperate rain forests are made up of a variety of tree species, including Douglas-fir, western hemlock, and western redcedar, it is the Sitka spruce that is the quintessential tree of this coastal "fog belt." It thrives equally well on wind-blasted headlands and in deep river valleys.

Growing along the coast from northern California to southern Alaska, Sitka spruce may grow up to 300 feet tall and 12 feet in diameter. These fast-growing trees will reach a height of 150 feet in 100 years, and 200-foot-tall specimens are common. Northwest Coast Indians weave the rootlets of Sitka spruce into baskets.

Cape Perpetua is an excellent place to see a coastal rain forest and its reigning monarch, the Sitka spruce. Managed by the Forest Service, 2,700-acre Cape Perpetua encompasses old-growth rain forest, rugged headlands, and rocky ocean shores. There is also overnight camping and a 19-mile, self-guided auto tour. Cape Perpetua Interpretive Center features exhibits on the environment, history, and native culture of the area.

Sitka spruce may grow up to 300 feet tall in the wet climate and fertile soils of the Pacific Northwest "fog belt."

The fun: For an intimate look at a fog-belt rain forest, hike the well-maintained Giant Spruce Trail. This trail, 2-miles round-trip, leads to a 500-year-old Sitka spruce. Pick up a self-guided interpretive brochure at the interpretive center. It describes the workings of an old-growth forest and is keyed to marked stations along the trail. Believe it or not, a rainy, foggy, winter day is the best time to see these forests because you can immerse yourself in the climate that created them.

There are nine other trails in the Cape Perpetua Scenic Area, ranging in length from 0.3 mile to 10 miles. They lead hikers through forest, to ocean views, and down to the sea's edge. You can pick up an information sheet on these trails at the interpretive center.

Food and lodging: Gas, lodging, food, and groceries are available in Yachats.

Next best: There are some excellent tidepools here. From the interpretive center, hike the paved 0.6-mile-loop Captain Cook Trail through dense vegetation and Indian shell middens (early Native American garbage dumps, where the empty shells of clams and mussels were thrown after the flesh was eaten) to the tidepools.

For more information:

Cape Perpetua Interpretive Center
Siuslaw National Forest
P.O. Box 274
Yachats, OR 97498
541-547-3289

The World Down Underwater 41

The wonders of the Pacific undersea world can be found under one roof here, from the smallest fish to frolicking seals and sea otters.

Site: Oregon Coast Aquarium, 1 mile (10 minutes) south of Newport.
Recommended time: Mid-December.
Minimum time commitment: 2 hours, plus driving time.
What to bring: Rain gear for wandering through the outside exhibits, camera with fast film for photographing on rainy days and through the underwater viewing windows of live exhibits.

Admission fee: $8.75 for adults, $7.75 for seniors, $4.50 for children 4 to 13. Children under 4 are admitted free.

Directions: From the south end of Newport, cross the Yaquina Bay Bridge via U.S. Highway 101. Just over the bridge, turn right at the sign for the aquarium. Turn right at the bottom of the exit and follow South Abalone Street about 0.3 mile to Southeast Ferry Slip Road. Go right on Southeast Ferry Slip Road and drive 0.2 mile to the aquarium parking area.

The background: You can find Oregon's ocean realm under one roof—and in the surrounding grounds—at the Oregon Coast Aquarium. The indoor portion of the aquarium features four galleries with displays on coastal waters, rocky shores, wetlands, and sandy shores. There are a variety of separate displays within each gallery. For example, the Sandy Shores Gallery has 13 different exhibits, including a 4,700-gallon tank that duplicates the marine environment around piers and docks. The draw at the Coastal Waters Gallery is the jellyfish exhibit. These otherworldly creatures float in slow motion in an acrylic cylinder 8 feet in diameter. There is also a learning lab, "touch pool," classroom, gift shop, café, and a theater that shows films of Oregon's whales and sharks.

Outside, 6 acres of live exhibits will introduce you to many of the common sea mammals and birds of the Oregon coast. These include exhibits of playful

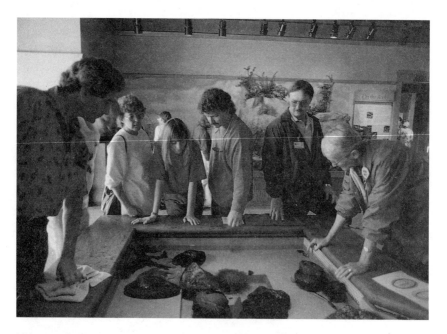

Visitors to the Oregon Coast Aquarium gather around a "touch pool" to get acquainted with creatures of the Pacific coast.

sea otters, seals, and sea lions. In the aviary, you can mingle with tufted puffins, common murres, and pigeon guillemots as they fly from rock to rock or swim deftly about in the water.

The fun: Start with the inside exhibits, where you will get close-up views of various denizens of the deep, as well as information about the lives of Oregon coastal sea creatures and the ecology of the ocean environment. The touch pool, where you can make the acquaintance of a variety of tidepool animals such as sea stars and anemones, is a fun place for both kids and adults to explore with curious fingers.

Next, move to the outside exhibits. Windows in artificial rock walls allow underwater views of seals and sea lions swimming about their tank—sometimes upside down. Be ready with your camera, because these are curious creatures and they often come right up to the window to have a look at you. At the sea otter exhibit, you can watch the animals swim on their backs on the surface, or you can see them cavort underwater from underwater viewing windows. Then join the free-ranging birds in the enclosed aviary. From this vantage, you will quickly see that seabirds, with their legs set far back on their body, were designed to swim, not walk. Waddling awkwardly on the rocks, they become graceful and confident as they slip into the aviary pool. If you need help while you are visiting, there is always an aquarium volunteer nearby to answer questions about the facility or the sea life that resides there.

Food and lodging: All services are available in Newport. There is a cafeteria-style restaurant at the aquarium.

Next best: A short trail leads from the aquarium to the nearby Mark O. Hatfield Marine Science Center. A center for important marine research, the facility also features aquarium exhibits and educational programs open to the public.

For more information:

Oregon Coast Aquarium
2820 SE Ferry Slip Road
Newport, OR 97365
541-867-3474

Wild Times in the City

Now while the summer crowds are gone, spend a winter's day on a worldwide wildlife safari in the heart of civilization.

Site: Oregon Zoo, 1.5 miles (10 minutes) from downtown Portland.
Recommended time: Mid-December.
Minimum time commitment: 3 hours, plus driving time.
What to bring: Rain gear, warm clothes, camera with telephoto lens.
Admission fee: $5.50 for ages 12 to 64, $4 for seniors 65 and older, $3.50 for children 3 to 11. Children under 3 are admitted free.
Directions: From downtown Portland, drive west on U.S. Highway 26 for about 1.5 miles. Take the zoo exit (1 mile after driving through the tunnel) and follow signs to the parking lot.
The background: Originally a small menagerie assembled as a hobby by a local pharmacist in the late 1800s, the Oregon Zoo became Portland's official zoo after the pharmacist donated his collection to the city. In 1987, the zoo celebrated its 100th birthday.

Today the Oregon Zoo occupies 64 acres within the Portland city limits, housing 200 species of animals and over 1,000 individual specimens. Nine major exhibits depict worldwide habitats and the wildlife that live in them. Among the exhibits are Alaskan Tundra, African Rainforest, African Plains, and Asian Elephants. Over 50 species of animals on display at the zoo are at risk of eventually becoming extinct in the wild.

The Oregon Zoo offers educational programs for a wide range of people, along with traveling exhibits that brings the zoo to communities around the state and annual events including festivals and concerts. The zoo is also involved in conservation programs to ensure the survival of wildlife species throughout the world.

Nearly 1 million people visit the Oregon Zoo each year. It is open every day except Christmas—from 9 A.M. to 4 P.M. from October 1 through March 31 and from 9 A.M. to 6 P.M. from April 1 through September 30.
The fun: While all the exhibits are fascinating, those featuring Northwest wildlife and environments are particularly interesting. They offer a chance to take a little excursion in the Cascade Mountains or Alaskan tundra at time of

This timber wolf is one of many fascinating species on display at the Oregon Zoo in Portland.

year when the real thing may be just a bit too cold.

Some of those exhibits include the elk meadow, where you can see bull and cow elk, and the Cascade Stream Exhibit, full of waterfowl and playful native river otters. The Great Northwest Exhibit, a work in progress, has opened with its first offering, the Cascade Crest Exhibit. It features mountain goats and the alpine environment in which they live. Eventually, this series of exhibits will depict wildlife and their habitats from the summit of the Cascade Mountains to the edge of the sea.

Food and lodging: Food is available on the zoo grounds. All services are available in Portland.

Next best: Stop at the World Forestry Center, across the parking lot from the zoo, to see exhibits about forestry and the forest environment.

For more information:

Oregon Zoo
4001 SW Canyon Road
Portland, OR 97231
503-226-1561

Out for the Count  43

Join local bird enthusiasts on a Christmastime outing to tally birds that spend the winter in the local vicinity. The information you gather will help conservationists monitor the long-term health of North American bird populations.

Site: National Audubon Society Christmas Bird Count, communities throughout Oregon.

Recommended time: Late December.

Minimum time commitment: A half day to a full day.

What to bring: Binoculars, bird guide, warm clothes, hiking boots, snacks, hot drinks.

Admission fee: None.

Directions: National Audubon Society chapters planning Christmas Bird Count outings post departure locations, dates, and times in local newspapers.

The background: In 1900, ornithologist Frank Chapman organized a Christmas bird count to protest a holiday event called a "side hunt," where teams of hunters went out and shot as many birds and small animals as possible. The team that killed the most creatures was declared the "winner."

Since that first count, local chapters of the National Audubon Society in the United States, Canada, Central and South America, the Caribbean, and even the Pacific islands get out each winter during the weeks just before and after Christmas to count the numbers and species of birds within a 15-mile circle over the course of a 24-hour period. Participants typically break up into teams that cover portions of the circle and then regroup in the evening to compile their observations. Over 45,000 people participate in this birding marathon each year.

The information garnered from the count is used to gauge the overall health of bird species that nest in North America as well as to give some insight into changes in the home ranges occupied by these species over the years.

The fun: Watch your local newspaper for notices of upcoming bird counts. They usually show up a week or so before Christmas. You can also contact your local National Audubon Society chapter directly.

While experienced birders are welcome, you do not have to be an expert to participate. The more birds spotted, the better the data. So the more eyes helping out, the better.

Sharp-eyed birders will spot a surprising number of species—perhaps even a gray jay like this one—during the annual Audubon Christmas Bird Count.

Food and lodging: Services will vary depending where your "counting circle" is located.

Next best: If you are not much of a cold-weather outdoors person, make a note on your calendar to get out for some birding when the weather turns balmy in the spring.

For more information:

Audubon Society of Portland
5151 NW Cornell Road
Portland, OR 97210
503-292-6855

A Host of Honkers 44

Canada geese gather by the thousands to spend the winter at this national wildlife refuge in the heart of the Willamette Valley.

Site: William L. Finley National Wildlife Refuge, 9 miles (15 minutes) south of Corvallis.

Recommended time: Early January.

Minimum time commitment: 3 hours, plus driving time.

What to bring: Rain gear, binoculars or spotting scope, field guide to birds, camera and telephoto lens.

Admission fee: None.

Directions: From Corvallis, drive south on Oregon Highway 99W for 8.2 miles. Turn right (west) onto Finley Refuge Road. Go 1.2 miles and turn left at the sign marking the refuge entrance. Continue 2.7 miles to the Display Pond parking area.

The background: This 5,325-acre refuge—a mix of farmland, forest, and wetland—is one of three national wildlife refuges established in the Willamette Valley in the 1960s to provide winter habitat for dusky Canada geese, a unique subspecies that is in decline due to habitat loss, hunting, and predation.

Dusky Canada geese nest in Alaska's Copper River Delta during the spring and summer and then spend winters in the Willamette Valley. The population of these birds has dropped from 25,000 in 1979 to about half that today. One of the major causes of the decline was the Alaskan earthquake of 1964, which raised the elevation of the Copper River Delta and made it less prone to flooding. This eliminated much of the wetland that dusky Canada geese rely on for nesting habitat. This also rendered their nests more vulnerable to foxes and other predators.

Other subspecies of geese found in the area during the winter include Taverner's Canada goose, cackling Canada goose, lesser Canada goose, western Canada goose, and Aleutian Canada goose.

The fun: First, stop at the interpretive kiosk 0.8 mile from the refuge entrance or at the refuge headquarters 1.6 miles from the entrance to pick up maps, brochures, and other information. Then proceed 1.1 miles beyond the headquarters to the Display Pond area. Drive slowly and watch the adjacent fields and Cabell Marsh to the southeast, because you will likely see flocks of geese resting in those areas. One of the best spots to see large concentrations of the birds is on the hillside to the right (west) just before you reach the Display Pond. Park at the Display Pond to scan the surrounding refuge lands.

Although the refuge is open year-round, most of it is closed to foot traffic from November 1 to April 30 to minimize disturbances of the wintering geese. During this time, you must remain in your vehicle within the core area of the refuge. Restricted areas are prominently signed. Viewing is best done from your vehicle anyway, because the geese will fly away if you open the car door.

Food and lodging: All services are available in Corvallis.

Next best: If you cannot visit during the prime period, geese are still present on the refuge, although in diminishing numbers, until late April.

For more information:

William L. Finley National Wildlife Refuge
26208 Finley Refuge Road
Corvallis, OR 97333
541-757-7236

Too Many Geese?

While thousands of geese sprawling across an open field or in full flight may be a beautiful thing to behold, it is possible to have too much of a good thing. Some believe that is the case with Canada geese in northwestern Oregon.

In the 1970s, about 25,000 Canada geese, most of them dusky, spent the winter in Oregon. They settled in areas ranging from the southern Willamette Valley north to the Columbia River, where the weather tends to be rainy but mild during that time of year. But the situation has since changed significantly. Today over 250,000 Canada geese may winter here. They sometimes cause considerable damage to farmers' fields by eating grain and other crops intended for market.

The reason for this increase is complex and involves a number of factors. With the exception of dusky Canada geese, populations of various subspecies once in decline have begun to increase due to conservation measures. In addition, the lush agricultural fields of northwestern Oregon provide perfect habitat for geese.

Each subspecies of goose that winters here has a different story. The cackling Canada goose population plummeted from 400,000 in the late 1960s to fewer than 25,000 by the mid-1980s due to hunting. The hunting season was temporarily closed for these geese in 1984, and their numbers soared. By 1993 there were about 164,000.

Taverner's Canada goose is the most common subspecies in this part of the state during the winter. Its numbers increased from about 3,000 in the 1960s to over 50,000 by the early 1990s, largely because of the rich food supply of winter wheat and rye grass available to them in agricultural areas.

The dusky Canada goose, which lost much of its nesting grounds on the Copper River delta as a result of the 1964 Alaskan earthquake, continues to have problems.

These subspecies of Canada goose, along with lesser, Vancouver, western, and Aleutian Canada geese, make up the different subspecies you will see during the winter in this part of the state.

As impressive as they are to watch, over a quarter million hungry geese descending on valuable croplands can cause economic losses for local farmers. And there are no simple answers. Hunting is often a good solution to controlling goose populations. But different subspecies of Canada geese can be difficult to identify at long distances, and wildlife managers worry that hunters may accidentally shoot dusky or Aleutian Canada geese, two subspecies whose populations are at risk. So hunters who want to hunt in areas where these two subspecies are found must first take a test to ensure that they are proficient in goose identification. ■

Secrets of the Winter Forest

Unlock the secrets of the winter wilderness and the creatures that manage to survive there while taking a guided snowshoe tour through the high country of the Cascade Mountains.

Site: Deschutes National Forest, 20 miles (30 minutes) west of Bend.
Recommended time: Early to mid-January.
Minimum time commitment: 1 hour, plus driving time.
What to bring: Camera, field guide to animal tracks, warm clothing, including hat, gloves, and boots. Dressing in layers is best, allowing you to add or subtract clothing depending on how cold it is and how much energy you expend while snowshoeing.
Admission fee: None.

The silence and solitude of the Cascade Mountains in winter belie the fact that life thrives here throughout the year.

Directions: From Bend, go west 20 miles on Century Drive, which eventually becomes Cascade Lakes Highway. Turn left at the turnoff for Mount Bachelor Ski and Summer Resort. Drive to the main parking area.

The background: The winter forest may seem still, empty, and far too inhospitable to sustain life. But life thrives here in the old-growth mountain hemlock forest near Mount Bachelor in the Deschutes National Forest.

The mountain hemlock zone is one of two subalpine ecological zones in the West where trees regularly grow 80 feet tall and reach 150 feet tall in old-growth areas (the other is the subalpine fir zone). Although deep snow and cold temperatures are the norm in this zone during the winter, many species of animals have adapted to life here. Snowshoe hares have large feet to keep them from sinking into the deep snow. American martens hunt in the tree-tops for Douglas squirrels. Hardy ravens, Clark's nutcrackers, and gray jays seem to be ever present, no matter what the weather. There is even activity beneath the snow, where mice and other small rodents build tunnels and move around out of sight of predators.

Each weekend from December through March, the Forest Service leads 1-mile interpretive snowshoe trips through an old-growth mountain hemlock forest near Mount Bachelor in the Deschutes National Forest.

The fun: Meet at the Mount Bachelor Ski and Sports Center on the south side of the parking lot. Trips leave at 10 A.M. and 1:30 P.M. During the course of the easy walk through the forest, guides explain the intricacies of winter ecology as you watch for wildlife and follow the tracks of snowshoe hares, American martens, and foxes. The guides also provide tips on traveling safely in the winter wilderness.

There is no need to register in advance. Trips are filled on a first-come, first-served basis. About 40 pairs of snowshoes are available free of charge.

Food and lodging: Food is available at Mount Bachelor Ski and Summer Resort. All services are available in Bend.

Next best: If snowshoeing sounds like too much work, or if you prefer a faster pace, guided interpretive cross-country and alpine ski tours are also offered at 10 A.M. and 3 P.M. respectively.

For more information:

Deschutes National Forest
Bend–Fort Rock Ranger District
1230 NE Third Street, Suite A262
Bend, OR 97701
541-388-5664

Ambling in an Ancient Forest 46

Wander through a splendid example of old-growth Douglas-fir forest that is accessible during the winter months, when many of Oregon's forests are locked in deep snow.

Site: Sandy River Gorge Preserve, 22 miles (40 minutes) east of Portland.
Recommended time: Mid-January.
Minimum time commitment: 4 hours, plus driving time.
What to bring: Rain gear, waterproof hiking boots, lunch, water.
Admission fee: None.
Directions: From Portland, drive east on Interstate 84 for 13 miles to Troutdale exit 17. Take this exit, pass the truck stop, and turn right onto 257th Avenue. Go 2.8 miles and turn left onto Southeast Division Street. Stay on Southeast Division Street (which eventually becomes Southeast Oxbow Road) for 4.8 miles. Bear right at the intersection and go 0.5 mile to Southeast Lusted Road. Turn left and drive 0.7 mile down a winding, steep grade. Turn left onto the small gravel road at the bottom of the grade and park at the gate 0.4 mile down the road.

Once thought to be beyond their prime, old-growth forests are in fact diverse and healthy ecosystems that harbor many species of wildlife.

The background: This 436-acre preserve, located in a 700-foot-deep gorge, protects one of Oregon's few remaining low-elevation, old-growth forests. Some of the trees are 500 years old. The preserve also protects a portion of the Sandy River—the last river near a metropolitan area on the west side of the Cascade Mountains that remains undeveloped. Designated a State Scenic Waterway in 1972 and a federal Wild and Scenic River in 1988, the Sandy River harbors runs of coho and chinook salmon, as well as steelhead. Its headwaters are on Mount Hood, 30 miles to the east.

The Nature Conservancy manages the area for its educational, natural, recreational, and scientific values. Staff members and volunteers maintain area trails, remove nonnative plants, and monitor water quality and fish habitat.

The fun: There is a sign along the road just inside the gate that offers an informative overview of the area and a basic trail map. From the trailhead, walk the 0.75-mile dirt road, called the River Road, into the gorge to the river. (Soon after leaving the trailhead, you will pass a private farmhouse and shed, so stay on the road.) There are plenty of big Douglas-firs to look at along the way. Once you reach the river, you can take Anne's Trail, which makes a half-mile loop through the forest and connects back to River Road, or you can return to your vehicle the way you came. Anne's Trail is not always well maintained, and you may need some basic route-finding skills to differentiate it from deer paths and other minor trails.

Although Sandy River Gorge Preserve is open to the public, it is owned by a private organization. Please respect the area, keep to the trails, and leave your dog at home for this excursion. The Nature Conservancy staff also asks groups of 10 or more to call their office before visiting the preserve.

Food and lodging: Food and lodging are available along Interstate 84 off exit 17.

Next best: During September and October, you can see chinook salmon spawning in the river here, as well as in Oxbow Regional Park just downstream.

For more information:

The Nature Conservancy of Oregon
821 SE 14th Avenue
Portland, OR 97214
503-230-1221

Forests Primeval

Forests of towering conifers comprise the quintessential image of the Pacific Northwest. Although much of Oregon's classic old-growth forest is gone, there are still remnants here and there, serving as habitat for species that require them and as reminders to humans of what once covered much of this part of the world.

At one time, an old-growth Douglas-fir forest, with trees in the 250- to 750-year-old range, was viewed as a dying forest. It was thought that these big trees were at the end of their lives, little new growth was taking place, and over time the entire forest would literally decay into nothing. But as scientists studied these forests, a different picture emerged.

The big trees in old-growth Douglas-fir forests are typically 400 to 500 years old, although some specimens may be over 1,000 years old and close to 300 feet tall. The forest canopy is multilayered, which means that the trees in these forests vary in size and age. There are huge, towering trees and young seedlings, as well as a variety of tree sizes in between. There are lots of downed logs, which decompose and serve as nurseries for new tree growth. Standing dead trees, or snags, provide homes for woodpeckers, flying squirrels, and other wildlife, while logs that have fallen into streams create habitat for trout and salmon, which hide and rest under them.

Because the habitat is so diverse, the wildlife population in old-growth forests is equally rich and varied. It includes northern spotted owls, American martens, red tree voles, goshawks, and Pacific giant salamanders. In fact, these types of forests support some 82 species of birds, 38 species of mammals, and 17 species of reptiles and amphibians. Many wildlife species found in old-growth forests require this unique habitat to survive.

In the wet Pacific Northwest, old-growth forests do their part to transfer moisture from sky to earth. The multilayered canopy collects moisture from fog. Then the water drips from the fir needles to the earth. In some areas, this "fog drip" may account for 30 percent of annual precipitation.

And as for the idea that an old-growth forest is a dying one, studies have shown that, overall, there is more new growth in these forests than dying, decaying trees.

But logging has taken a toll on the region's old-growth forest, which two centuries ago covered an estimated 15 million acres of the Pacific Northwest. Scientists estimate that, today, only about 10 percent of these ancient forests remain. ■

Out to Pasture

A resident herd of 35 to 45 Roosevelt elk spend the winter in the pasture of this former ranch before heading to the high country for the summer.

Site: Walton Ranch Interpretive Trail, 20 miles (30 minutes) east of Sweet Home.

Recommended time: Late January.

Minimum time commitment: 45 minutes, plus driving time.

What to bring: Warm clothes, spotting scope or binoculars, camera with telephoto lens.

Admission fee: None.

Directions: From Sweet Home, drive 20 miles east on U.S. Highway 20. Watch the right side of the road for the Trout Creek Trail sign, 0.1 mile past Trout Creek Campground, which is also on the right. The trailhead is directly across the road from the trail sign, on the left (north) side of the highway.

The background: Large herds of Roosevelt elk wander the western slopes of the Cascade Mountains throughout the year. Yet most people seldom have an opportunity to see this animal of the wilderness high country. From spring through fall, the elk range through mountain meadows and deep forests. But

Walton Ranch Interpretive Trail

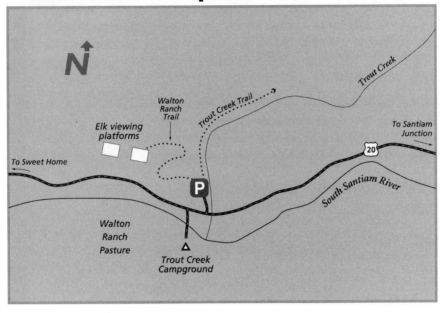

during the winter, heavy snows and cold weather drive them to lower elevations, where they seek milder temperatures and areas with little or no snow
covering the grasses and forbs they feed on.

The pasture of the abandoned Walton Ranch, along the South Santiam
River, is one place where wintering elk can reliably be seen during the winter.
Located right on the edge of the snow line, the pasture is often free of snow,
even though it may be storming just a few miles up the road. This allows the
elk easy access to the nutritious grass they need to carry them until spring,
when they disperse once again to the high country.

The fun: A 0.1-mile trail begins at the west end of the trailhead parking lot.
The wide, gravel trail is barrier free, and there are benches along the way if
you need to stop and rest. The trail climbs to a double platform and walkway
with expansive views of the pasture below.

From the platforms, scan the pasture with a spotting scope or binoculars
for elk standing and feeding or lying down. If you do not see any elk in the
middle of the meadow, carefully scan the edges of the forest that encircles it.
Often, the elk congregate at one end of the pasture.

Food and lodging: The Mountain House, off US 20, 3.6 miles east of the
trailhead, has a restaurant and small grocery store. There is no gas. All services are available in Sweet Home.

Next best: Hike the 2.4-mile Trout Creek Trail into the Menagerie

The observation platform at the end of the Walton Ranch Interpretive Trail provides expansive views of the surrounding meadow and the Roosevelt elk that graze there.

Wilderness Area. The trail leads to the ridgetop high above and a collection of rock spires named after various animals. How far you get will depend on how much snow has fallen.

For more information:
Willamette National Forest
Sweet Home Ranger District
3225 Highway 20
Sweet Home, OR 97386
541-367-5168

Waterfowl Winter

Tens of thousands of migrating ducks and geese gather on this reservoir in the Columbia River basin each winter.

Site: Cold Springs National Wildlife Refuge, 7 miles (10 minutes) east of Hermiston.

Recommended time: Late January.

Minimum time commitment: 3 hours, plus driving time.

What to bring: Binoculars or spotting scope; field guide to birds; warm, waterproof clothing; waterproof boots.

Admission fee: None.

Directions: From U.S. Highway 395 in Hermiston, go east on East Highland Road, which becomes East Loop Road in about 1 mile. Continue on East Loop Road for 5.5 miles and then turn left onto Reservoir Road and into the wildlife refuge. Go 0.4 mile on Reservoir Road, bear left at the fork, and continue 1.4 miles to Lot B.

The background: This 3,112-acre wildlife refuge is managed by the U.S. Fish

Cold Springs National Wildlife Refuge

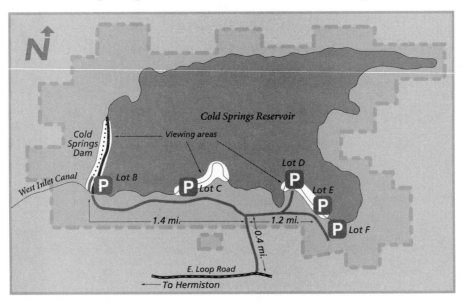

and Wildlife Service and is strategically positioned to provide winter habitat for migrating waterfowl in the Columbia River basin. The centerpiece of the refuge is Cold Springs Reservoir, which furnishes irrigation water to surrounding farms during the summer. At full capacity, the reservoir holds 1,550 surface acres of water, but by August, the demand for irrigation has reduced it to just 200 surface acres of water.

Nevertheless, during the winter, the area plays host to up to 45,000 ducks and geese, which depend on the reservoir's open water as a resting place during their migration south. In addition to open water, the wetlands and shrub-steppe uplands also found on the refuge provide important habitat for many other species of wildlife throughout the year.

The fun: Park at Lot B and walk through the gate at the west end of the lot. Follow the trail along West Inlet Canal and cross the canal over a concrete bridge. The trail is about 200 yards long, and it leads to a gravel road (no vehicles permitted) on Cold Springs Dam along the west shore of the reservoir. From here, you have expansive views of the open water as well as of flooded timber and brush along the southern shore. Your best bet is to find a comfortable spot, settle in, and scan the open water with binoculars and spotting scopes to see how many species of ducks you can identify. As many as 20

The 1,550-acre Cold Springs National Wildlife Refuge provides a winter refuge for tens of thousands of ducks, geese, and other migrating waterfowl.

Roadmap in the Sky

The fact that birds can find their way across thousands of miles of seemingly trackless sky as they migrate between summer and winter grounds is one of the wonders of the natural world.

For some species, simply flying in the right direction for a certain amount of time gets them close enough to their ultimate destination that they can divine the rest of the way using local landmarks. For others, migratory navigation is more complex than you might think.

There are three basic compasses birds use to navigate their migration routes: a star compass, sun compass, and magnetic compass. Lodged just above a bird's nostrils are small magnetite crystals, which allow the bird to detect magnetic north and therefore orient itself to the four cardinal directions.

Birds are also able to navigate by the stars, detecting the center of rotation of the constellations relative to the earth's rotation. Currently, that point is Polaris, the North Star, but it changes over the millennia because

the earth pivots on its axis due to the gravitational pull of the moon and sun. For that reason, it is more useful for birds to learn to recognize the star's rotation point rather than the position of the North Star. Someday the North Star will not be the North Star anymore.

A bird's internal clock, which allows it to determine the sun's location in relation to the time of day, enables it to figure the four directions. Birds may also be able to understand that the sun rises in the east and sets in the west to help them fix their position in the sky.

Other ways birds may find their way across long distances include sounds, smells, landscape characteristics, and, for ocean-going migrants, wave patterns that may suggest that land is near.

Whatever the navigational method, migratory birds find their way across immense distances and over massive mountain ranges and vast oceans on their perpetual journeys each year between northern breeding grounds and southern winter sanctuaries. ■

different species of ducks pass through here during winter migration.

You can also search the coves and flooded timber along the southern shore of the reservoir. To do so, park at Lot C, D, or E, all of which are accessible along the main entrance road. You will pass Lot C on the way to Lot B. To reach Lots D and E, bear right at the fork on Reservoir Road. Park and walk along the southern edge of the reservoir.

The wildlife refuge is open year-round from 5 A.M. to 1.5 hours after sunset. At that time, the entrance gate to the refuge automatically closes, so be sure you leave the refuge before then. Portions of the refuge are closed through-out the year to protect wildlife. Other areas are closed from October 1 through the end of February, so observe the closure signs.

Food and lodging: All services are available in Hermiston.

Next best: Other wildlife refuges in the Columbia River basin where you can see large numbers of wintering waterfowl include Umatilla National Wildlife Refuge and McKay Creek National Wildlife Refuge. You can get information about visiting these areas by contacting the address and phone number below.

For more information:

Mid-Columbia River National Wildlife Refuge Complex
P.O. Box 700
Umatilla, OR 97882
541-922-3232

Deer Diner

Mule deer by the hundreds gather in a roadside field to graze during the cold desert winter.

Site: Oatman Flat, 39 miles (45 minutes) south of La Pine.

Recommended time: Early February.

Minimum time commitment: 30 minutes, plus driving time.

What to bring: Binoculars or spotting scope, camera with telephoto lens, warm clothing.

Admission fee: None.

Directions: From Bend, drive south on U.S. Highway 97 for about 28 miles to La Pine. Just south of town, turn left (southeast) onto Oregon Highway 31 and go 39 miles. Oatman Flat is on the right (west). It is marked by a wildlife viewing sign and a small turnout.

The background: Mule deer inhabit the open woodlands and mountain ranges of eastern Oregon and are a common sight in this part of the state. Often, they live in groups led by an older doe.

During the summer, mule deer range throughout the mountain country. But when temperatures drop and snow begins to fall, they begin to descend into the valleys, seeking milder weather conditions and less snowpack in order to reach grass and other forage.

At this time of year, mule deer are often spotted in herds along highways and near towns. A favorite winter refuge for these animals is crop and pasture

When winter hits the high country, mule deer head down the mountain to ranchers' fields for free meals of alfalfa and other hay crops.

land, where they sometimes eat a good portion of the hay intended for domestic livestock.

One area where you can see large numbers of mule deer congregating is Oatman Flat, a 100 acre alfalfa field right along the side of the road. As many as 500 to 1,000 mule deer may gather here during the winter, making for quite a wildlife spectacle.

The fun: Park at the turnout and scan the field for deer. Mornings and evenings see the most activity and the most animals, but there may be deer there at any time of the day. Remember that the field is private property, so do not trespass.

Food and lodging: Food, groceries, and gas are available in Silver Lake, 8 miles south of Oatman Flat. All services are available in La Pine.

Next best: Winter is a good time to look for hawks and eagles at Fort Rock State Natural Area. Stop on your way to or from Oatman Flat. The natural area is 29 miles south of La Pine (10 miles north of Oatman Flat) and 7.5 miles east from OR 31. There are signs directing you there.

For more information:

Oregon Department of Fish and Wildlife
36981 Highway 31
Summer Lake, OR 97640
541-943-3152

Waterworld

A spectacular array of waterfalls in all their power and splendor awaits winter hikers along the Trail of Ten Falls, just outside Oregon's capital city.

Site: Silver Falls State Park, 23 miles (40 minutes) east of Salem.

Recommended time: Mid-February.

Minimum time commitment: 5 hours, plus driving time.

What to bring: Rain gear, waterproof hiking boots, lunch, drinking water, camera with telephoto lens.

Admission fee: Daily visitor permits are $3 per vehicle. A season pass, which is good for all Oregon State Parks, is $25.

Directions: From Salem, drive east on Oregon Highway 22 for 7 miles. Turn north onto OR 214 and follow it 16 miles to the South Falls Day Use Area on the left. Park at the north end of the parking lot and follow the signs to the lodge and South Falls trailhead.

The background: At 8,700 acres, Silver Falls State Park is the largest in the Oregon State Park system. Nestled in a forest of Douglas-firs and western hemlocks, the park offers camping, an interpretive program, convention facilities, and a historical lodge, built in the 1930s, which now serves as a visitor center.

But the primary draw for visitors is the series of 10 waterfalls that plummet over steep cliffs along the course of Silver Creek. They range in height from 27 feet to 178 feet. During the wet winters in western Oregon, they are in their prime.

The creation of the Silver Creek gorge goes back about 26 million years to a time when most of western Oregon was inundated by the Pacific Ocean. About 15 million years ago, the waters receded. The sandstone that had formed at the bottom of the ocean was then covered by lava flows from Cascade volcanoes and undersea vents. Over the succeeding centuries, erosion carved out the canyon. Softer rock behind several of the falls has eroded, allowing hikers to view the falls from an unusual perspective.

The fun: Before you begin your hike of the Trail of Ten Falls (and there really are 10: South, Lower South, Lower North, Double, Drake, Middle North, Twin, North, Upper North, and Winter), pick up a trail map at the visitor center, housed in the historical lodge. Take the short paved trail behind the lodge to

South Falls is one of a spectacular array of waterfalls along the Trail of Ten Falls in Silver Falls State Park.

the South Falls Trailhead. From the trailhead, the trail drops quickly to the base of South Falls, where you have the option of either crossing the creek or walking behind the falls. As you continue on the Trail of Ten Falls, you hike through the canyon past eight falls and reach the North Falls Day Use Area, where you connect with the 2.5-mile Rim Trail. From the North Falls Day Use Area, you can take the easy 0.2-mile gravel trail to Upper North Falls. Then double back to the Rim Trail and continue on to Winter Falls. The Rim Trail loops back to the South Falls Day Use Area.

Food and lodging: All services are available in Salem. There is a snack bar and nature store at the lodge. The park has three campgrounds with developed and undeveloped sites.

Next best: If the full 7.2-mile hike is too rigorous for you, there are two trails that branch off the main trail and return to the visitor center. These allow you to shorten the hike to 2.3 or 5 miles.

For more information:
Silver Falls State Park
20024 Silver Falls Highway
Sublimity, OR 97385
503-873-8681

Eagles Everywhere 51

Learn all about bald eagles as you watch hundreds fly from their roosts in the Klamath Basin, home of the largest winter concentration of these magnificent birds in the contiguous United States.

Site: Klamath Basin Bald Eagle Conference, Oregon Institute of Technology, Klamath Falls and Bear Valley National Wildlife Refuge, 140 miles (2.75 hours) south of Bend, 365 miles (5.5 hours) southeast of Portland.

Recommended time: Mid- to late February.

Minimum time commitment: 1 to 3 days.

What to bring: Binoculars or spotting scope, field guide to birds, camera with telephoto lens, warm clothing.

Admission fee: $20 to $80, depending on which seminars, lectures, and field trips you sign up for.

Directions: To reach Klamath Falls from Bend, drive south on U.S. Highway 97 for 137 miles. From Portland, go south on Interstate 5 for 280 miles to

Medford. At Medford, take exit 30 and go north on Oregon Highway 62 for 6 miles. Turn east onto OR 140 and go 78 miles to Klamath Falls.

The background: Up to 800 bald eagles spend November through March in the Klamath Basin after migrating from as far away as the Northwest Territories, Saskatchewan, and interior British Columbia. It is the largest winter concentration of bald eagles in the lower 48 states. While in the basin, the raptors feed on the waterfowl that also migrate through here during the winter.

Since 1979, the Klamath Basin Bald Eagle Conference has been held in Klamath Falls on President's Day weekend (the second or third weekend of February) to help people learn more about eagles and their natural history and conservation. The conference features a variety of activities, including lectures and seminars about bald eagles presented by scientists and other experts and classes on wildlife drawing, bird identification, fly-tying, and crafts— as well as socializing, entertainment, and a banquet.

Conference highlights include field trips to watch eagles fly from their night roosts in Bear Valley. Participants may see anywhere from 100 to 300 eagles within a few hours. Typically, 300 to 500 people attend the conference each year.

The fun: Call or write ahead for registration materials and sign up to attend the Bald Eagle Conference. Several registration options are available depending on how much time you have available and how much you want to spend. Even though many scientists give talks at the conference, the entire event is geared toward nonscientists who are interested in learning about, and seeing, bald eagles.

Food and lodging: All services are available in Klamath Falls. Conference attendees must make their own lodging arrangements.

Next best: If you want to look for eagles on your own, you can often see them from the roads in the Worden area, 13 miles south of Klamath Falls on US 97. The best time to look is from just before to just after sunrise. Bear Valley National Wildlife Refuge is just west of Worden. The refuge is closed to the public from November through April to avoid disturbing wintering eagles.

For more information:
Bald Eagle Conference
c/o Klamath County Department of Tourism
P.O. Box 1867
Klamath Falls, OR 97601
800-445-6728

Return of a Symbol

The United States adopted the bald eagle as its national symbol in 1782. But by 1981, 90 percent of the nesting pairs of these birds were located in just 10 states. By 1982, there were just 1,500 bald eagles in the nation outside of Alaska.

The culprits in the precipitous decline of these great American birds were many: habitat destruction, bounty hunting, collisions with power lines, and, significantly, the use of pesticides—DDT in particular.

Just after World War II, DDT began to be used widely as a pesticide in this country. In the late 1940s, a retired banker and bird enthusiast named Charles Broley began banding and studying bald eagles on the Florida Gulf Coast. Soon, he began noticing that an increasing percentage of nesting eagles failed to successfully hatch any eaglets. By the late 1950s, he had documented a significant decline in the number of young eagles successfully hatched along the Gulf Coast. During the same time period, scientists discovered that DDT could result in sterility in some animals and that these effects could be passed up the food chain—to predators like the bald eagle. DDT sprayed onto cropland was eventually washed into rivers, streams, and lakes, where it was absorbed by aquatic plants and small aquatic creatures, which were then eaten by fish. The eagles got the pesticide into their systems when they ate contaminated fish—their primary food source. And this was happening all over the country, not just in Florida.

Before Broley died, he alerted the National Audubon Society to this chemical threat, which had the ability to drive the eagles to extinction. In response, the society began a conservation effort to help the birds. Further research, in a cooperative effort between the National Audubon Society and the U.S. Fish and Wildlife Service, determined that DDT was impairing the eagles' ability to produce eggs with strong shells. Instead, female eagles laid thin-shelled eggs that broke when they tried to incubate them. The impact on eagle populations was serious. By the early 1960s, there were fewer than 450 pairs of nesting bald eagles in the lower 48 states. There were just 20 nesting pairs in Oregon. Bald eagles were declared an endangered species (except in Alaska, which had a healthy bald eagle population) in 1967 under the federal Bald Eagle Protection Act, the precursor to the Endangered Species Act of 1973. The use of DDT was banned in 1972.

Since that time, the conservation effort to save the species has paid off. Today there are about 4,500 nesting pairs of bald eagles in the lower 48 states, including over 300 in Oregon. There are also numerous immature birds. By 1999, the bald eagle had recovered to the point that the federal government was considering removing it from the Endangered Species list. ■

Eagle Alley

Up to 100 bald eagles, some coming from as far away as Canada's Northwest Territories, spend the winter in the upper Crooked River basin along with resident golden eagles. You can see them perched on trees and rock ledges or soaring majestically in the sky above.

Site: Upper Crooked River Basin, 26 miles (30 minutes) southeast of Prineville.

Recommended time: Late February.

Minimum time commitment: 4 hours, plus driving time.

What to bring: Warm clothing, binoculars or spotting scope, camera with telephoto lens, field guide to birds or raptors, hot drinks, snacks.

Admission fee: None.

Directions: From Prineville, go east for 1 mile on U.S. Highway 26. Turn right (south) onto the Paulina Highway and drive 25 miles to Post, where the best viewing begins. The 22-mile Beaver Creek Loop is about 30 miles east of Post. To get there, continue past Post for 26 miles to Paulina. A couple of miles past Paulina, bear left onto County Road 113. Go another 2 miles and turn right onto Pruitt Road (County Road 135), which follows Beaver Creek, eventually connecting with Forest Service Road 58. At this junction turn left (west) and continue on until you rejoin CR 113.

Upper Crooked River Basin

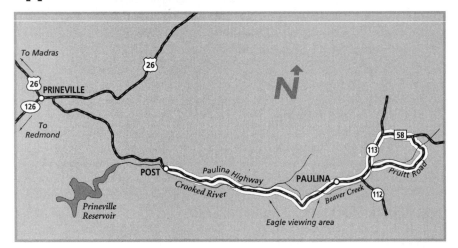

Golden eagles are a common sight along the upper Crooked River, east of Prineville.

The background: Up to 100 bald eagles migrate from their summer grounds in the Northwest Territories to Washington and gather along the upper Crooked River to spend the winter. During this time, they roost for the night in trees, fly to feeding areas in the morning, and return to their roosts at dusk. Although bald eagles are typically fish eaters, they often feast on dead waterfowl, road-killed deer, and other carrion in inland wintering areas such as this.

Equally impressive golden eagles, which reside in the area year-round, are visible along the highway as well.

The fun: Drive the Paulina Highway to the Beaver Creek Loop, watching for eagles as you go. Look for them perched in trees along the road, soaring above, and even sitting in fields and pastures. Since much of this country is open, you usually have good, unobstructed views.

The best time to be here is between 9 A.M. and 3 P.M., when the bald eagles leave their roosts and fly about in search of food. The eagles pick their roosting trees based on how protected they are from winter weather.

To spot golden eagles, you should watch for them soaring along the cliffs or perching on rugged crags.

Food and lodging: All services are available in Prineville. Gas and groceries are available in Post.

Next best: Other nearby places to look for bald eagles are Lake Billy Chinook, west of Madras; Ochoco Reservoir, just east of Prineville; and along Oregon Highway 126 between Prineville and Redmond.

For more information:

Bureau of Land Management
3050 NE Third Street
Prineville, OR 97754
541-416-6700

Best Bets

Best Trips for Families

1 Desert on Display
3 Thar She Blows
4 A Trillion Trilliums
12 Salamander Central
22 Marine Garden Bounty
23 Up and Over
25 Journey to the Stars
26 Landscapes Frozen in Time
32 The Long Journey Home
33 The Hues of Autumn
40 Rainy Day Rain Forest
41 The World Down Underwater
42 Wild Times in the City
47 Out to Pasture

Best Trips for Birders

2 Great Blue Commune
5 Dance of the Sage Grouse
9 Spring Has Sprung
10 Desert Oasis
11 Owl Watching Is a Hoot
15 Seabird Condo
16 Water Bird Way Station
31 Raptors on the Wing
39 Shorebird Sanctuary
43 Out for the Count
44 A Host of Honkers
48 Waterfowl Winter
51 Eagles Everywhere
52 Eagle Alley

Best Trips for Hikers

4 A Trillion Trilliums
6 In the Fire's Wake
7 A Cacophony of Camas
8 Bloom with a View
9 Spring Has Sprung
20 Alpine Bouquet
27 Ice Is Nice and Will Suffice
36 The Working Forest
37 Shifting Sands
38 Wetlands at Work
40 Rainy Day Rain Forest
45 Secrets of the Winter Forest
46 Ambling in an Ancient Forest
50 Waterworld

Best Trips for Photographers

4 A Trillion Trilliums
5 Dance of the Sage Grouse
7 A Cacophony of Camas
8 Bloom with a View
10 Desert Oasis
16 Water Bird Way Station
17 Elk in Repose
19 Butterfly Byway
20 Alpine Bouquet
22 Marine Garden Bounty
27 Ice Is Nice and Will Suffice
28 Grand Views in a Big Country
33 The Hues of Autumn

Best Trips for a Rainy Day

1   Desert on Display
23   Up and Over
34   Going Underground
40   Rainy Day Rain Forest
41   The World Down Underwater
42   Wild Times in the City
50   Waterworld

Trips to See Wild Animals

3   Thar She Blows (gray whales)
12   Salamander Central (rough-skinned newts)
14   Bright River, Big Bugs (salmonflies)
17   Elk in Repose
18   Snakes Alive (garter snakes)
19   Butterfly Byway
21   Seals on the Rocks (harbor seals)
23   Up and Over (steelhead)
24   Where the Deer and the Antelope Play
29   Elk in Love
30   Kokanee on Parade
32   The Long Journey Home (spawning salmon)
47   Out to Pasture (Roosevelt elk)
49   Deer Diner (mule deer)

Trips to See Flowers

4   A Trillion Trilliums
7   A Cacophony of Camas
8   Bloom with a View
13   Come into My Parlor, Said the Flower to the Fly
20   Alpine Bouquet

Easiest Trips

12   Salamander Central
13   Come into My Parlor, Said the Flower to the Fly
17   Elk in Repose
21   Seals on the Rocks
44   A Host of Honkers

Driving Tours

10   Desert Oasis
16   Water Bird Way Station
19   Butterfly Byway
26   Landscapes Frozen in Time
28   Grand Views in a Big Country
33   The Hues of Autumn
35   Record in the Rocks
52   Eagle Alley

Most Scenic Trips

3   Thar She Blows
8   Bloom with a View
20   Alpine Bouquet
22   Marine Garden Bounty
24   Where the Deer and the Antelope Play
26   Landscapes Frozen in Time
27   Ice Is Nice and Will Suffice
28   Grand Views in a Big Country
31   Raptors on the Wing
33   The Hues of Autumn
37   Shifting Sands
45   Secrets of the Winter Forest
50   Waterworld

Best Trips for the Mobility Impaired

Index

About the Author

An Oregon resident for 25 years, author Jim Yuskavitch lives on the east slope of the Cascades, just outside the small town of Sisters. He is a full-time writer and photographer who specializes in natural history and the environment.

FALCON GUIDES® Leading the way™

FalconGuides® are available for where-to-go hiking, mountain biking, rock climbing, walking, scenic driving, fishing, rockhounding, paddling, birding, wildlife viewing, and camping. We also have FalconGuides on essential outdoor skills and subjects and field identification. The following titles are currently available, but this list grows every year. For a free catalog with a complete list of titles, call FALCON toll-free at 1-800-582-2665.

BIRDING GUIDES

Birding Illinois
Birding Minnesota
Birding Montana
Birding Northern California
Birding Texas
Birding Utah

PADDLING GUIDES

Floater's Guide to Colorado
Paddling Minnesota
Paddling Montana
Paddling Okefenokee
Paddling Oregon
Paddling Yellowstone & Grand

WALKING

Walking Colorado Springs
Walking Denver
Walking Portland
Walking St. Louis
Walking San Francisco
Walking Virginia Beach

CAMPING GUIDES

Camping Arizona
Camping California's
   National Forests
Camping Colorado
Camping Southern California
Recreation Guide to Washington
   National Forests

FIELD GUIDES

Bitterroot: Montana State Flower
Canyon Country Wildflowers
Central Rocky Mountain
   Wildflowers
Great Lakes Berry Book
New England Berry Book
Ozark Wildflowers
Pacific Northwest Berry Book
Plants of Arizona
Rare Plants of Colorado
Rocky Mountain Berry Book
Scats & Tracks of the Pacific
   Coast States
Scats & Tracks of the Rocky Mtns.
Southern Rocky Mountain
   Wildflowers
Tallgrass Prairie Wildflowers
Western Trees
Wildflowers of Southwestern Utah
Willow Bark and Rosehips

ROCKHOUNDING GUIDES

Rockhounding Arizona
Rockhounding California
Rockhounding Colorado
Rockhounding Montana
Rockhounding Nevada
Rockhound's Guide to
   New Mexico
Rockhounding Texas
Rockhounding Utah
Rockhounding Wyoming
Teton National Parks

HOW-TO GUIDES

Avalanche Aware
Backpacking Tips
Bear Aware
Desert Hiking Tips
Hiking with Dogs
Mountain Lion Alert
Reading Weather
Route Finding
Using GPS
Wilderness First Aid
Wilderness Survival
Zero Impact

MORE GUIDEBOOKS

Backcountry Horseman's
   Guide to Washington
Family Fun in Montana
Family Fun in Yellowstone
Exploring Canyonlands & Arches
   National Parks
Exploring Hawaii's Parklands
Exploring Mount Helena
Exploring Southern California
   Beaches
Hiking Hot Springs of the Pacific
   Northwest
Touring Arizona Hot Springs
Touring California & Nevada
   Hot Springs
Touring Montana and Wyoming
   Hot Springs
Trail Riding Western Montana
Wild Country Companion
Wilderness Directory
Wild Montana
Wild Utah
Wild Virginia

■ *To order any of these books, check with your local bookseller*
*or call FALCON ® at **1-800-582-2665**.*
Visit us on the world wide web at:
www.FalconOutdoors.com

FALCON®

FALCONGUIDES ®Leading the Way™

HIKING GUIDES

Best Hikes Along the Continental Divide
Hiking Alaska
Hiking Arizona
Hiking Arizona's Cactus Country
Hiking the Beartooths
Hiking Big Bend National Park
Hiking the Bob Marshall Country
Hiking California
Hiking California's Desert Parks
Hiking Carlsbad Caverns
   and Guadalupe Mtns. National Parks
Hiking Colorado
Hiking Colorado, Vol. II
Hiking Colorado's Summits
Hiking Colorado's Weminuche Wilderness
Hiking the Columbia River Gorge
Hiking Florida
Hiking Georgia
Hiking Glacier & Waterton Lakes National Parks
Hiking Grand Canyon National Park
Hiking Grand Staircase-Escalante/Glen Canyon
Hiking Grand Teton National Park
Hiking Great Basin National Park
Hiking Hot Springs in the Pacific Northwest
Hiking Idaho
Hiking Indiana
Hiking Maine
Hiking Maryland and Delaware
Hiking Michigan
Hiking Minnesota
Hiking Montana
Hiking Mount Rainier National Park
Hiking Mount St. Helens
Hiking Nevada
Hiking New Hampshire
Hiking New Mexico
Hiking New Mexico's Gila Wilderness

Hiking New York
Hiking North Carolina
Hiking the North Cascades
Hiking Northern Arizona
Hiking Northern California
Hiking Olympic National Park
Hiking Oregon
Hiking Oregon's Eagle Cap Wilderness
Hiking Oregon's Mount Hood/Badger Creek
Hiking Oregon's Central Cascades
Hiking Pennsylvania
Hiking Ruins Seldom Seen
Hiking Shenandoah
Hiking the Sierra Nevada
Hiking South Carolina
Hiking South Dakota's Black Hills Country
Hiking Southern New England
Hiking Tennessee
Hiking Texas
Hiking Utah
Hiking Utah's Summits
Hiking Vermont
Hiking Virginia
Hiking Washington
Hiking Wisconsin
Hiking Wyoming
Hiking Wyoming's Cloud Peak Wilderness
Hiking Wyoming's Teton
   and Washakie Wilderness
Hiking Wyoming's Wind River Range
Hiking Yellowstone National Park
Hiking Yosemite National Park
Hiking Zion & Bryce Canyon National Parks
Wild Country Companion
Wild Montana
Wild Utah
Wild Virginia

■ *To order any of these books, check with your local bookseller*
or call FALCON ® at **1-800-582-2665**.
Visit us on the world wide web at:
www.Falcon.com

FALCON®

FALCONGUIDES ® Leading the Way™

FALCONGUIDES ® are available for where-to-go hiking, mountain biking, rock climbing, walking, scenic driving, fishing, rockhounding, paddling, birding, wildlife viewing, and camping. We also have FalconGuides® on essential outdoor skills and subjects and field identification. The following titles are currently available, but this list grows every year. For a free catalog with a complete list of titles, call FALCON® toll-free at 1-800-582-2665.

MOUNTAIN BIKING GUIDES

Mountain Biking Arizona
Mountain Biking Colorado
Mountain Biking Georgia
Mountain Biking Idaho
Mountain Biking New Mexico
Mountain Biking New York
Mountain Biking North Carolina
Mountain Biking Northern New England
Mountain Biking Oregon
Mountain Biking Pennsylvania
Mountain Biking South Carolina
Mountain Biking Southern California
Mountain Biking Southern New England
Mountain Biking Utah
Mountain Biking Washington
Mountain Biking Wisconsin
Mountain Biking Wyoming

LOCAL CYCLING SERIES

Mountain Biking Albuquerque
Mountain Biking Bend
Mountain Biking Boise
Mountain Biking Chequamegon
Mountain Biking Chico
Mountain Biking Colorado Springs
Mountain Biking Denver/Boulder
Mountain Biking Durango
Mountain Biking Flagstaff and Sedona
Mountain Biking Grand Junction & Fruita
Mountain Biking Helena
Mountain Biking Moab
Mountain Biking Phoenix
Mountain Biking Spokane and Coeur d'Alene
Mountain Biking the Twin Cities
Mountain Biking Utah's St. George/Cedar City Area
Mountain Biking the White Mountains (West)

■ *To order any of these books, check with your local bookseller or call FALCON ® at **1-800-582-2665**.*
Visit us on the world wide web at:
www.Falcon.com

FALCON®

FALCONGUIDES® Leading the Way™

FALCONGUIDES® are available for where-to-go hiking, mountain biking, rock climbing, walking, scenic driving, fishing, rockhounding, paddling, birding, wildlife viewing, and camping. We also have FalconGuides® on essential outdoor skills and subjects and field identification. The following titles are currently available, but this list grows every year. For a free catalog with a complete list of titles, call FALCON® toll-free at 1-800-582-2665.

SCENIC DRIVING GUIDES

Scenic Driving Alaska and the Yukon
Scenic Driving Arizona
Scenic Driving the Beartooth Highway
Scenic Driving California
Scenic Driving Colorado
Scenic Driving Florida
Scenic Driving Georgia
Scenic Driving Hawaii
Scenic Driving Idaho
Scenic Driving Indiana
Scenic Driving Kentucky
Scenic Driving Michigan
Scenic Driving Minnesota
Scenic Driving Montana
Scenic Driving New England
Scenic Driving New Mexico
Scenic Driving North Carolina
Scenic Driving Oregon
Scenic Driving the Ozarks
Scenic Driving Pennsylvania
Scenic Driving Texas
Scenic Driving Utah
Scenic Driving Virginia
Scenic Driving Washington
Scenic Driving Wisconsin
Scenic Driving Wyoming
Scenic Driving Yellowstone and
    the Grand Teton National Parks
Scenic Byways East & South
Scenic Byways Far West
Scenic Byways Rocky Mountains
Back Country Byways

WILDLIFE VIEWING GUIDES

Alaska Wildlife Viewing Guide
Arizona Wildlife Viewing Guide
California Wildlife Viewing Guide
Colorado Wildlife Viewing Guide
Florida Wildlife Viewing Guide
Indiana Wildlife Viewing Guide
Iowa Wildlife Viewing Guide
Kentucky Wildlife Viewing Guide
Massachusetts Wildlife Viewing Guide
Montana Wildlife Viewing Guide
Nebraska Wildlife Viewing Guide
Nevada Wildlife Viewing Guide
New Hampshire Wildlife Viewing Guide
New Jersey Wildlife Viewing Guide
New Mexico Wildlife Viewing Guide
New York Wildlife Viewing Guide
North Carolina Wildlife Viewing Guide
North Dakota Wildlife Viewing Guide
Ohio Wildlife Viewing Guide
Oregon Wildlife Viewing Guide
Puerto Rico & the Virgin Islands
    Wildlife Viewing Guide
Tennessee Wildlife Viewing Guide
Texas Wildlife Viewing Guide
Utah Wildlife Viewing Guide
Vermont Wildlife Viewing Guide
Virginia Wildlife Viewing Guide
Washington Wildlife Viewing Guide
West Virginia Wildlife Viewing Guide
Wisconsin Wildlife Viewing Guide

HISTORIC TRAIL GUIDES

Traveling California's Gold Rush Country
Traveling the Lewis & Clark Trail
Traveling the Oregon Trail
Traveler's Guide to the Pony Express Trail

■ *To order any of these books, check with your local bookseller*
or call FALCON ® at ***1-800-582-2665***.
Visit us on the world wide web at:
www.falcon.com

FALCON®

FALCONGUIDES ® Leading the Way™

www.Falcon.com

Since 1979, Falcon® has brought you the best in outdoor recreational guidebooks. Now you can access that same reliable and accurate information online.

❒ <u>Browse our online catalog</u> for the latest Falcon releases on hiking, climbing, biking, scenic driving, and wildlife viewing as well as our Insiders' travel and relocation guides. Our online catalog is updated weekly.

❒ A <u>Tip of the Week</u> from one of our guidebooks or how-to guides. Each Monday we post a new tip that covers anything from how to cross a rushing stream to reading contour lines on a topo map.

❒ A chance to <u>Meet our Staff</u> with photos and short biographies of Falcon staff.

❒ <u>Outdoor forums</u> where you can exchange ideas and tips with other outdoor enthusiasts.

❒ Also <u>Falcon screensavers and panoramic photos</u> of spectacular destinations.

And much more!

Plan your next outdoor adventure at our web site. Point your browser to www.Falcon.com and get FalconGuided!

FALCON®